The Proven Winners Garden Book

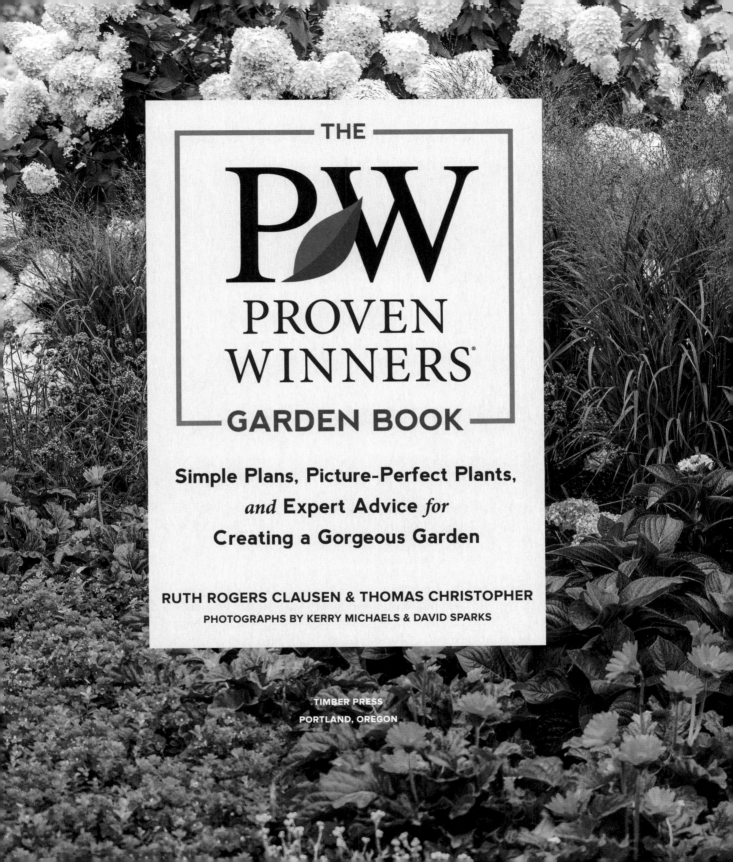

THE

PW

PROVEN WINNERS®

GARDEN BOOK

Simple Plans, Picture-Perfect Plants, *and* Expert Advice *for* Creating a Gorgeous Garden

RUTH ROGERS CLAUSEN & THOMAS CHRISTOPHER
PHOTOGRAPHS BY KERRY MICHAELS & DAVID SPARKS

TIMBER PRESS
PORTLAND, OREGON

Frontispiece: This colorful garden's mixture of annuals (verbenas, dwarf morning glories, gerbera daisies, strawflowers) and perennials (summersweet, hydrangeas, and switch grasses) is hardy enough to tolerate the climatic challenges of coastal locations and the Southwest.

▶ The inky black foliage of Sweet Caroline Bewitched After Midnight sweet potato vine.

Published in 2019 by Timber Press, Inc.
The Haseltine Building
133 S.W. Second Avenue, Suite 450
Portland, Oregon 97204-3527
timberpress.com

Printed in China.

Text design by Laura Shaw Design

Library of Congress Cataloging-in-Publication Data

Names: Clausen, Ruth Rogers, 1938- author. | Christopher, Thomas, author.
Title: The proven winners garden book: simple plans, picture-perfect plants, and expert advice for creating a gorgeous garden / Ruth Rogers Clausen, Thomas Christopher; photographs by Kerry Michaels and David Sparks.
Description: Portland, Oregon: Timber Press, 2019. | Includes index. | Identifiers: LCCN 2018020838 (print) | LCCN 2018027217 (ebook) | ISBN 9781604698978 () | ISBN 9781604697551 (pbk.)
Subjects: LCSH: Gardening.
Classification: LCC SB450.97 (ebook) | LCC SB450.97 .C53 2019 (print) | DDC 630.2/515—dc23
LC record available at https://lccn.loc.gov/2018020838

A catalog record for this book is also available from the the British Library.

THIS BOOK HOPES TO PROVIDE ENCOURAGEMENT
TO THOSE STARTING ON THE GARDENING PATH.

Contents

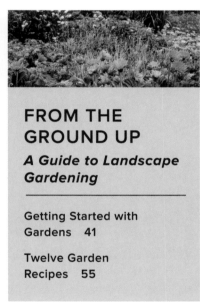

◀ Foliage plants such as Prairie Winds Cheyenne Sky red switch grass and 'Black Pearl' coral bells provide an artistic backbone to designs when flowers fade.

Introduction
Recipes for Success

With this book, beautifying your home landscape has never been easier—or more economical and fun. Forget all the complications of gardening rules and jargon; we've simplified this process to a series of straightforward recipes, like your favorite cookbook. Follow the step-by-step instructions and you'll find that success comes just as surely outdoors as in the kitchen, as you quickly transform the ordinary into something truly special.

As with cooking, the success of your garden depends on the quality of the ingredients you use. Proven Winners has devoted years to collecting and testing plants, seeking varieties that not only produce the most attractive flowers and foliage, but which are also the most reliable and durable performers. All are outstandingly vigorous, disease-free, and the best of their kind in coping with stresses such as extreme heat and drought. The plants in these recipes are also easy to grow: most are compact, and so can stand on their own without troublesome staking and with a minimum of pruning.

You'll find detailed introductions to creating both in-ground gardens and gardens in containers. Part one starts with the basics—selecting a spot, designing a garden, shopping for plants—that apply to any type of garden and any type of gardener. The second part is dedicated to landscape gardening. Before delving into the twelve recipes, with themes such as fragrant combinations and shady retreats, read up on everything from preparing the soil to keeping your garden healthy down the road. Next, the container section: a trove of twenty-five enticing designs along with the container-specific know-how for getting your plants happily situated in their pots (or urns, baskets, bowls, and more). Simple planting

◀ This garden attracts the eye but not four-legged pests, with its flush of vibrant deer-resistant annuals: Luscious Berry Blend lantana, Diamond Frost euphorbia, and Supertunia Sangria Charm.

▶ Coordinated containers can transform an outdoor space instantly. And when it comes to attracting butterflies—as this combination of verbenas, bidens, and lantanas is designed to do—two containers are more effective than one.

schematics and plentiful photos combine to present a full picture of how to do it and what beauty the end result will offer.

Interwoven throughout the book are tips for saving money and techniques that make the job easier—tricks of the trade that we learned from the pros. We understand that your time *and* money are both precious. With this book, you'll economize on both, almost certainly earning back the cost of this book and more with the first landscape project you undertake. To that point, a variety of studies have found that good landscaping can add 10 percent or more to the value of your home. So while enhancing your own satisfaction and pleasure in your home, you can at the same time boost its curb appeal.

USING THE RECIPES IN THIS BOOK

Everyone's situation is different and so are their tastes. That's why we've made these recipes easy to adapt. It's your choice: you can use the recipes in this book as a blueprint for your planting—plug them right into your landscape—or as a starting point for developing your own plans. Maybe you'll need to adjust a recipe to better suit your local climate, or maybe you want it to better reflect your plant preferences. In either case, these recipes are calculated to encourage creativity; we've recommended substitutions for the various ingredients to help you customize each recipe, if that is your desire.

Keep in mind that the plants in each of the thirty-seven recipes, including the recommended substitutes, have been selected for their compatibility. That is, all plants in a given recipe thrive in the same degree of sun, in a similar climate, and with a comparable degree of moisture. They are also aesthetically compatible—within the same recipe the plants work together in color, texture, and fragrance to create a whole that is greater than, and more beautiful than, the parts. If, for any reason, you cannot find the recommended plants or substitutes at your local garden center, you can use another Proven Winners plant of the same type. So, for example, if you cannot find Infinity Pink New Guinea impatiens, you can substitute Infinity Pink Frost or even Infinity Dark Pink or Infinity Salmon Bisque. Lastly, if you choose to include or substitute plants beyond the ones recommended in the book, just be sure that they are compatible with the other elements of the recipe.

Above all, this process is about trusting yourself and your instincts. If you've ever decorated a house or even just a room, you already have many of the skills you need to make your homescape attractive, comfortable, and colorful. This book will help you harness those skills and provide the technical support you'll need to express yourself in greenery and flowers. It's your garden after all, and should reflect your taste and please you, fitting your lifestyle and the needs of your family.

A Winning Garden

MASTERING THE BASICS

SELECTING A SPOT

Choosing an appropriate site for your planting is the essential first step. This decision depends partly on aesthetics—you'll want to locate your planting in a prominent and visible spot where it will have maximum impact. You'll also want to make sure that the site provides optimum conditions for the growth of the plants.

ON THE LEVEL

Ideally, the spot you select should be level, so that precipitation and irrigation water soak into the ground, rather than running down and off across a sloping surface. It is often possible to tell whether a site is approximately level simply by eye or by watching what happens to water that falls there. For a more exact reading, hook an inexpensive mason's line level (obtainable at any hardware store or home center) onto the center of a length of strong string, and stretch it between stakes driven into the ground on either side of your proposed planting area. Tie the string to the stakes at the same height on either end, and the line level will show you if the string is level with the ground below it.

If the site is markedly sloping, you can create a level planting area by installing a retaining wall of landscape timbers of sufficient height on the downhill side. Or you can make a series of level planting areas by terracing—framing raised beds with landscape timbers, lumber, or flat rocks. Using wood that has been pressure-treated with a preservative ensures that your construction will be long lasting.

◄ A hot and sunny spot is both challenge and boon. But with appropriately tough plants and proper care, your garden will thrive. Here, dark-leaved Mystic Illusion dahlias are balanced with Rockin' Playin' the Blues salvias, Goldilocks Rocks bidens, and Supertunia Vista Fuchsia petunias.

Preparing the Soil

Unless you are very lucky, the soil in your yard will need some work before it is ready for planting. Usually, you will need to dig up the planting area to relieve soil compaction, and aerate the soil so it can absorb moisture and foster root growth. This also creates an opportunity to add organic matter, such as compost or sphagnum peat, and fertilizers to the soil. Preparing soil for a garden planting differs considerably from preparing potting mix for container plantings. For a detailed discussion of these processes, see pages 42 and 144 in the introductions to landscape and container gardening, respectively.

▲ A sunny spot is best for a spring-themed hanging basket of pansiolas, lobelias, and nemesias.

SUN VS. SHADE

Sun is the fuel for plant growth, and different types of plants require different octanes, different strengths, of sunlight. Plants that need exposure to unfiltered sunlight throughout most of the day (6 hours or more) to thrive are labeled as requiring "full sun" or "sun." Others perform best when exposed to sunshine for just part of the day (4–6 hours) and are labeled "part sun" or "part shade" (sometimes called partial sun or partial shade). Still others adapt best to conditions excluding direct light—the label on these will specify "full shade" or "dense shade."

How much sun does your potential planting site receive daily in summer? Check it several times throughout the day—it can help to take snapshots—and refer to the table on the following page to ascertain whether conditions qualify as full sun, part shade/part sun, or full shade.

Use a compass or your smartphone to determine what direction your garden faces. Sites on the south side of a house or on a south-facing slope are the sunniest and tend to be hot and dry, good candidates for drought-resistant plantings. The soil here also warms earlier in the season. North-facing sites tend to be cooler with less intense sunlight, and even if exposed to full sun throughout the day are usually suitable for part shade plants. Morning sun (found in spots that face east) is less intense than afternoon sun (found in spots facing west); a site that receives sunlight only in the morning is good for plants designated for part shade to shade, while a spot that is exposed to the sun through the afternoon is better suited to plants labeled for part shade to sun.

▼ Under the canopy of an established tree (*Cornus mas*), shade-loving plants such as hostas, browallias, torenias, and New Guinea impatiens thrive. The bench offers a cool and peaceful resting place for gardeners and thinkers.

ASSESSING YOUR SITUATION

HOURS OF SUNLIGHT RECEIVED PER DAY	EXPOSURE (DIRECTION FROM WHICH SUNLIGHT COMES)	PLANT ADAPTATION AND SITE NOTES
6 or more hours of direct sunlight	South or west	**Full sun plants** *South-facing sites are hottest and typically favor drought-resistant plants; west-facing sites are hottest in early afternoon.*
6 or more hours of direct sunlight	East or north	**Full or part sun plants** *Sunlight is less intense here so such sites tend to be cooler; suitable for plants that ordinarily flourish in part sun.*
4–6 hours of direct sunlight	South or west	**Part sun plants** *This site favors plants that can tolerate some shade as well as heat and strong sunlight.*
4–6 hours of direct sunlight	East or north	**Part shade plants** *This site is better suited to shade-tolerant plants.*
Dappled light filtered through overhanging canopy of branches	East, west, or south	**Part shade plants** *Light is strongest in the spring before trees leaf out; especially appropriate for spring-blooming bulbs but also suitable for plants such as hostas that require less light.*
No direct light		**Full or dense shade plants** *This site is suitable for only the most shade-tolerant plants; such sites are often drought-prone because rain is blocked by overhanging structures and/ or moisture is drawn from soil by roots of overhanging trees and shrubs.*

SEASONAL DIFFERENCES

Because the sun rises higher in the sky in summer than in winter, patterns of sun and shade in your yard will change, often markedly, with the passage of the seasons. In general, shadows cast by objects (such as buildings) or evergreens to the south of your garden will extend farther in wintertime, including a greater area in their shade. Off-setting this is the fact that deciduous trees and shrubs lose their leaves in wintertime, allowing sunlight to penetrate areas that are shaded in the summer.

Sun in Southern Regions

The summer sun is more intense in the southern regions of North America, and southerners will find that some shade during the midday hours can actually be beneficial even for plants labeled as adapted to full sun. If the intensity of the sun is too much for a particular plant, typically it will display burning or crisping on the margins of the upper leaves.

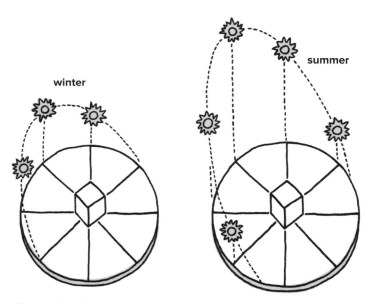

▲ The sun's path across the sky varies throughout the year, and at different times of day.

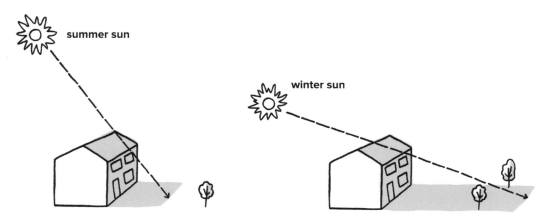

▲ The sun is considerably higher in the sky in summer than in winter. This means that the shadow cast by the house during the summer is shorter than the shadow cast in winter.

THE EFFECT OF WIND

An airy site is, in general, healthy for plants. A gentle breeze dries foliage more quickly after rain or irrigation and blows away fungal spores, thus reducing the danger of disease. However, constant exposure to strong winds, as on an unsheltered hilltop, is likely to be harmful. Frequent strong winds dehydrate plants, and are especially dangerous to evergreens in wintertime (wind burn can severely damage foliage, potentially killing the plant). Wind can also physically damage plants, breaking or deforming trunks and branches, and tearing leaves.

If your garden is wind-prone, consider installing a windbreak on the side that faces into the prevailing wind. Erecting a solid fence or wall is the quickest but not always the soundest solution. Although such a structure blocks the wind from the area immediately in its lee, it actually increases air turbulence farther downwind. A permeable barrier such as trellising, a slatted or louvered fence, or a windbreak of mixed shrubs and/or evergreens, is more effective at taming the wind. Typically, this provides an area of calm in its lee extending three times as far as the height of the barrier or windbreak.

▶ A solid structure blocks the wind from the area immediately in its lee, but air turbulence further downwind increases.

▶ A permeable windbreak that allows air to pass through while reducing its speed—such as this mixture of trees and shrubs of varying heights—is most effective.

Microclimates

Within your yard there are likely to be areas where the climate differs significantly from that of its surroundings. The area at the foot of a sun-drenched, south-facing wall, for example, is likely to be warmer than its surroundings, even in wintertime. Conversely, a location on a north-facing slope is likely to be cooler and more frost-prone, due to receiving less direct sunlight (at least in the Northern Hemisphere, where the sun comes from the south). An area adjacent to a pond or stream—thanks to the moderating effect of the water—is likely to be cooler than its surroundings in the summertime and milder in the winter.

An important skill for gardeners is to recognize and make use of such aberrations. A warmer microclimate, for instance, provides an opportunity to successfully grow plants that are marginally winter-hardy in your region. A cooler microclimate provides an opportunity to grow annuals that find the heat (and often accompanying high humidity) of mid-summer overly oppressive.

Recognizing microclimates depends on careful observation. Watch for areas where the frost or snow melt first to identify warmer microclimates. An area where the grass browns prematurely in the summer suggests that this is a dry, and perhaps hot, microclimate. If nothing else, recognizing that the typical garden is a patchwork of microclimates can help you understand why some plants flourish in one area and not in another.

WATER

When selecting a spot for planting, make sure that a water source is conveniently near at hand. Most plants need some irrigation during the summer—annuals, with less extensive root systems, tend to need more frequent watering than deeper-rooted perennials. Established shrubs that root deeply can often tolerate a significant drought, but all grow and look better with at least weekly deep watering during hot, dry weather. See page 49 for more information on the different devices and irrigation systems you can use to water your garden.

Container plantings will likely need daily (or sometimes twice daily) watering in summertime. Whatever your irrigation schedule, however, dragging hoses or heavy, filled watering cans far distances will make this activity an unpleasant and time-consuming chore. It is wise to plan the location of your planting before you get too far along in the process or design and installation. Make sure it is within easy range of a water source, be it a stand pipe, water barrel, or hose extension.

DEMYSTIFYING DESIGN

This book includes many recipes—so how do you choose the ones best suited to your yard? The answer, of course, depends on your personal style. The secret to creating a space in which you are comfortable is to make your yard an honest expression of who you are and what you like. This is also the key to giving your landscape the sort of personal flavor that makes it interesting to others. You may find in these pages just the recipes you need, but you should also feel free to treat them as starting points, extracting ideas that you incorporate into your own original design.

Also remember that you don't have to limit yourself to a single style. You may, for example, adopt a more formal design for the front yard entrance to your home, and an informal one to frame the backyard terrace where you like to entertain. Similarly, a planting of tropical exuberance may seem best suited poolside; closer to the house, you may want something more restrained. As you leaf through the recipes and find the ones that suit your fancy, keep these design basics in mind.

◄ Let your inner designer weigh in on garden decisions. If you tend to choose brightly colored clothes or home decor, you may especially enjoy the bold blooms of Toucan Rose canna lily and Summerific Perfect Storm hibiscus in this tropical combination.

EASY CLUES

Design is a word that intimidates most home landscapers—having never thought of themselves as designers, they don't know where to begin. But the fact is that you, like everyone else, have already developed a personal style.

First, look in your clothes closet, and you'll see which colors you favor. Do you prefer soft pastels or bold, bright hues? Do you like clothes with a daring, innovative cut, or do you prefer the timeless appeal of traditional styles? Take

▲ Elevated on a pedestal in the garden, this pink-themed container pops. The variety of texture and habit—from the arching Fireworks red fountain grass to the Superbena Sparkling Ruby—add interest and drama.

these preferences into the landscape and the result will fit you as well as your favorite suit—or jeans.

Another clue to garden design lies in taking a good look around your home. How have you furnished your house? Do you lean toward the clean simple lines of Scandinavian-modern furniture? Then a stripped-down minimalist look is likely to be the one for your garden. Or do you prefer the cozy exuberance of a country look? You'll probably feel most comfortable with a colorful and informal planting. If you feel at home with a French Provincial–style living room, consider similar formality in your garden. Reflecting your individual style in your garden or container will elevate it from the routine to the personal.

If your landscaping efforts complement the style of your house, they will have far more impact. For example, a simple four-square pattern of beds provides a historically authentic entrance to a colonial; a cottage-garden-style potpourri of flowers enhances the intimate charm of a bungalow or Cape Cod house. On the other hand, a formal Japanese-style garden would clash with a historic cottage, though it may perfectly suit the spare aesthetic of contemporary architecture.

An additional point to keep in mind as you work on your design is what you hope to gain from your garden. Do you want lots of flowers to cut for the house? Then be sure you have space for a cutting garden. Do you want to entertain on a back porch decorated with flashy tropical plants or long-blooming annuals in hanging baskets? Go for it. Are you a budding or accomplished chef? You will probably want an herb garden near the kitchen door, or a container of culinary herbs by the back door or alongside the barbeque grill. Remember that this is your garden, and it should reflect your preferences.

PRACTICAL MATTERS

Few of us possess unlimited budgets, and so designing the landscape becomes a matter of figuring out what we can do with what we've got. Here are a few important points to consider while planning your landscape.

MONEY

One way to create a luxurious landscape on a limited financial budget is to divide the property into a number of separate manageable projects—such as front yard, backyard, side yard, deck, or patio. Some people prefer to start by working on the most visible area, such as the front entryway, embarking on other projects as money becomes available. Alternatively, you may want to hold off on the bigger, more visible areas until you've gained more experience and confidence, and tackle the less-prominent areas first.

TIME

In your enthusiasm for having a garden, it can be easy to go overboard, designing a space that you don't have enough time or energy to care for. Before you begin, make an honest and conservative assessment of the time you will have available on a regular basis for maintenance. If small children and a demanding job leave you with very little leisure, consider limiting your plantings to containers and hanging baskets, which, after installation, require only a few minutes daily for watering and other maintenance. By starting small you will avoid planting a garden that becomes a chore, or worse, an eyesore.

WORKING WITH WHAT'S THERE

Use the existing shrubbery and trees as a framework for your design. Tucking colorful flowers in the ground or in containers around and among your foundation plants can give the entryway a look of instant maturity. You can also provide established shrubs with a new look (if desired) by selective pruning. Clipped azaleas gain a more natural profile by snipping out branches here and there, and allowing the remaining ones to grow freely. Conversely, you can give a shaggy evergreen a more formal look by trimming it to a symmetrical profile with hedge clippers. For new plantings, always consider the mature size of the plants. It is not uncommon to see overgrown foundation shrub plantings that have almost swallowed the residence. Pruning takes time, or money to hire professionals, so select shrubs and trees to be in scale for their chosen spots.

REPETITIVE ELEMENTS

In the same way that you might color-coordinate outfits with accessories, such as a tie, belt, or scarf, you can repeat a color or plant type in several places in the garden. This selection can be either as a mass or a single specimen, but be sure to make it a bold enough statement that it has a visual impact. You can readily explore this principle with a container planting. Experiment with using just one sweet alyssum for example, as opposed to planting three or four. It will be obvious that a single plant alone generally produces little impact. There are exceptions to this rule, however. For example, even a single weeping Japanese maple, because of its size and beauty, is sufficient to make a focal point in a garden.

Likewise, you can employ garden accessories to create effects. Typically, such objects are placed singly, to serve as centerpieces and focal points. You can also use them in multiples, though, to create a rhythm. Try placing a succession of planters or other objects at intervals along a path or throughout a bed—it can help to tie the whole design together and lead the eye from point to point through the landscape.

◀ The pink blooms in the featured container (Supertunia Vista Bubble-gum) are repeated in the cluster of additional planters on the far side of the pool, uniting the scene.

USING FOLIAGE TO ENHANCE DESIGN

At first glance, colorful flowers are usually what dominates and attracts our attention. But really they are just the icing on the cake. Foliage is just as important to a plant design, both in containers and in the ground. Indeed, the leaves of a plant may be more important in the long run. After the flowers fade, the foliage must hold a design together until the next flush of bloom. Here are some tips that apply to both container designs and those planted in the ground.

- We tend to think of leaves as "just green" but fail to appreciate the silvery gray-greens of lavenders, the blue-greens of some catmints, and the yellow-greens of sedums. Plant combinations offer additional design benefits: The silvery leaves of Russian sage highlight the deep purple flowers of calibrachoa, while the deep orange foliage of a coral bells plant can put a brighter shine on a cluster of orange gerbera daisy flowers. And remember that colors don't always remain the same through the season. Some foliages are one color when the plant emerges in spring and then turn another as they mature in summer, and many plants have foliage that changes color dramatically in the fall before the leaves drop.

▲ A monochromatic melding of Supertunia Really Red, Superbells Red calibrachoa, and Superbena Scarlet Star.

▲ A complementary pairing of blue (Blue My Mind dwarf morning glory) and orange (gerbera daisies and Luscious Marmalade lantana) flowers.

Many of the recipes showcase a particular color palette, including all-white, all-blue, or all-red blossoms, which can enhance an arrangement's impact. The impression of purity, for instance, is even greater with a collection of three or four types of white flowers than with one. Such monochromatic arrangements also highlight differences in texture between the plants, thus enriching the appeal in that important respect. Other recipes include flowers and foliage of different hues and textures selected for their visual compatibility. Still others contrast flower colors such as blue and orange, creating a strong visual statement that can energize a scene.

- Contrasting foliage textures within a design keep it interesting. Try putting ferns next to hostas or prickly hollies alongside broad-leaved 'Limelight' hydrangea. Consider adding tall wavy grasses to provide height and movement to contrast with mounding or trailing petunias.

- Variegated foliage is usually a standout and ideal for visual focal points in your garden or container planting. Along with hostas, consider Jade Peacock foamflower and My Monet weigela. Their showy leaves attract attention all season.

- Another dimension to explore is using shrubs with interesting or colorful bark. This is especially effective for gardens or containers that are viewed and enjoyed in the wintertime. Vibrant red- or yellow-stemmed dogwoods, for example, are especially valuable for winter gardens where they complement the deep greens of evergreens. Oakleaf hydrangeas and crape myrtles both display exfoliating or peeling bark. This is more apparent when the leaves have dropped and the trunk is more easily visible.

ACCESSORIZING YOUR GARDEN

As you look through the recipes, you will find that some include decorative items, such as a birdbath, bench, or urn. These accessories can be personal. As an example, you might want to display treasures collected on vacation. If you are a potter, sculptor, or artist in another medium it's fun to site special items as focal points, maybe at the end of a walkway or to flank a doorway.

Where is there a particularly fine view? This may be the wider landscape or "borrowed view" beyond your property (a hillside, river, or coastline perhaps) or it could face back towards the house, or direct the eye to a particularly fine specimen tree. Celebrate the vista with a viewing bench or seat, but be sure that it is a comfortable perch for friends. Sitting areas can be open or private, the latter perhaps for meditation.

What's critical is that the surrounding plantings are in scale with the particular decoration. Be sure that overly large shrubs do not overwhelm a delicate-looking sculpture, or an assertive, oversized garden ornament does not dwarf the surrounding plantings. Embellish your garden "rooms" with appropriate accessories, but be careful not to clutter the garden with too much stuff. Coordination and scale among the elements is important.

The focal point (sculpture) of the design on the left is too small and cluttered by the busy plantings. By contrast, a larger sculpture with the same plantings is more proportional.

On the left, a busy, uncoordinated cluster of ornaments loses its impact; in contrast (right) to fewer items and a larger focal point carefully placed and in scale for greater appeal.

◄ Surround bird-related accessories such as birdhouses or birdbaths with plants that provide cover, nesting space, or berries. This attractive birdbath, which makes a statement without overwhelming the planting, is a welcome addition to a garden designed to attract songbirds. Dark cherry pink bee balm, white summer snapdragons, and golden-colored perennial sunflowers are among the features.

SHOPPING FOR PLANTS

The recipes in this book are filled with three types of plants: shrubs, annuals, and perennials. A shrub (or bush) is a woody plant smaller than a tree, usually having multiple permanent stems branching from or near the ground. This category includes such landscaping favorites as rhododendrons, azaleas, roses, and hydrangeas. Shrubs add structure to a planting and serve as a graceful and imposing background. Trees are also woody, but they are usually confined to single major trunk or stem. Unless a building plot has been cleared for building, it is likely that at least a few existing trees on the property will help shape your garden plans.

Annuals and perennials are plants without woody stems. Annuals grow, bloom, and set seed within a single season or just part of a growing season, and then die. Perennials, under suitable conditions, survive and bloom from one year to the next. Some perennials (coral bells, for example) are evergreen, keeping their foliage through the winter. More commonly, however, perennials go dormant and die back to their crowns or roots in the fall, hide underground over the winter, and then send up new shoots come spring.

On the face of it, perennials, with their repeated encores, seem the best buy for flower-lovers. However, during their short lifespan, annuals usually bloom far more prolifically than perennials. Most perennials are genetically programmed to bloom for a set period, usually two to several weeks, at the same time each year. Annuals, in contrast, literally bloom themselves to death, flowering continuously until the plant produces seed or it is cut down by adverse weather (frost, heat, drought). If you break the cycle by removing the flowers as soon as each blossom starts to age and wilt (a practice known as deadheading), your annuals

◄ Mystic Illusion dahlias are frost-sensitive perennials with an enticing contrast of star-shaped yellow flowers and dark foliage.

will continue to bloom for months of color. You'll find that many Proven Winners annuals are self-cleaning—that is, the fading flowers drop naturally from the plants. This self-cleaning characteristic not only improves the appearance of the plant, but it also eliminates the need for deadheading.

To achieve a similarly long-lasting display with perennials, you must plant early-season bloomers, as well as those that provide color in mid-season and later into fall, so that as one perennial is finishing, another is ready to flower. Creating a display with perennials alone requires more planning and patience. Most take a year or more of settling into their new home and becoming established before they put on a good floral display. Experienced gardeners often choose to intermingle annuals with perennials: use perennials to create a permanent backbone or structure for the display, but tuck in annuals around them to add splashes of summer-long color.

HARDINESS ZONES

When planning a new design for the yard, it is tempting to focus solely on choosing flowers that look beautiful together. In our preoccupation, it is easy to lose track of an incredibly important aspect of good design: the plants we select must be adapted to our local conditions. Beauty and good health, after all, go hand in hand—even the most beautiful flower loses its appeal when the plant is struggling to survive in unsuitable conditions.

Because annuals survive only for a single growing season, they aren't affected by winter cold and can flourish in a broad range of climates. Shrubs and perennials, however, are more dependent upon climate and it is important to make sure that the ones you select are suited to your region. You do this by determining your local climate zone—you'll find a map at planthardiness.ars.usda.gov/PHZMWeb/ that gives climate zones for the entire United States. These zones are based on the lowest temperature experienced in each region in an average winter, from the coldest, Arctic zone 1 to the warmest, tropical zone 13. Typically, you'll find a range of zones listed on plant labels (except on annuals), listing where the plant in question is hardy, with the lower number indicating winter hardiness. For example, a plant rated for zones 7–11 is hardy only through zone 7 (where winter lows on average drop to 0 to 10°F.); it will not survive the cold of zone 5 (where winter lows on average reach -20 to -10°F), whereas a plant rated for zones 5–9 will be fine.

SUMMER HARDINESS

It isn't just winter cold that challenges plants. Summer heat, especially when combined with humidity as in the Southeast, threatens their health as well. Many of the annuals sold in springtime, such as pansies and trailing lobelias, thrive in cool, moist weather, but quickly fade during the hot days of summer. Southern gardeners are likely to find that such traditional spring plantings fare better in their climate when planted in mid- to late fall for a winter display.

Still other plants, such as sweet alyssum, petunias, calibrachoas, and bidens, may survive hot summer weather but cease blooming when experiencing such stress. Fortunately, the plant breeders who furnish plants for Proven Winners have developed new, heat-tolerant selections of such plants.

Commonly, gardeners will find an indication about summer hardiness in the range of zones recommended for a plant on its label. For example, North Pole arborvitae is described as hardy from zones 3–7; this means that this evergreen will survive winters anywhere in this range, and summers too. That is, the plant is summer hardy as far south as USDA zone 7, but not, in a typical year, in the next zone south (zone 8).

When considering summer hardiness, remember that typically the challenge to plants is the combination of summer heat with humidity, and that plants may prove to be more heat tolerant in drier (less humid) climates. The same plant that expires in the heat and humidity of a zone 8 summer in the eastern half of North America may well flourish in the dry heat of a western zone 8, as long as it receives sufficient irrigation.

▲ Populated with selections of tough dahlias, petunias, and sweet potato vine, this container will withstand the high temperatures of summer.

Read the Plant Tag

The series (Superbells) and variety (Coralberry Punch) name of the plant

How much sun or shade this plant needs to grow

How tall you can expect the plant to grow

SUPERBELLS®
CORALBERRY PUNCH

FULL TO PART SUN   8-12"

Calibrachoa hybrid

The plant's Latin or botanical name

Download FREE app for more
planting ideas and information at
www.provenwinners.com/scan

QR code: Scan this code with your smartphone for a plant fact sheet, more growing information, combination ideas, and photos

16

Most of the information you need to choose appropriate plants, suitable to your region and your particular yard, are right at hand on the plant tag you'll find slipped into nursery pots and packs. Learning to decipher that information is an essential skill. Don't forget to turn the plant tag over: an astounding amount of detailed growing information is packed into this small surface.

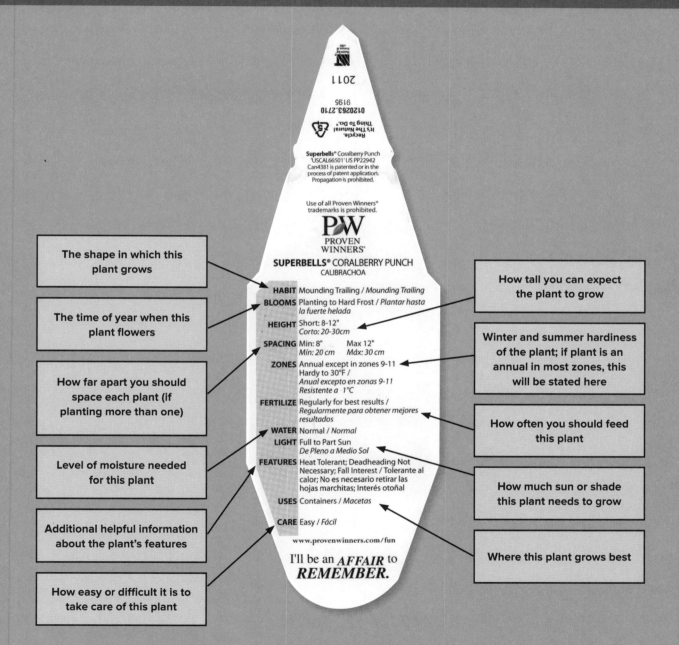

The shape in which this plant grows

The time of year when this plant flowers

How far apart you should space each plant (if planting more than one)

Level of moisture needed for this plant

Additional helpful information about the plant's features

How easy or difficult it is to take care of this plant

How tall you can expect the plant to grow

Winter and summer hardiness of the plant; if plant is an annual in most zones, this will be stated here

How often you should feed this plant

How much sun or shade this plant needs to grow

Where this plant grows best

2011

9195
0120263.2710

Recycle.
It's The Natural
Thing To Do.®

Superbells® Coralberry Punch
'USCAL66501' US PP22942
Can4381 is patented or in the
process of patent application.
Propagation is prohibited.

Use of all Proven Winners®
trademarks is prohibited.

PW
PROVEN
WINNERS®

SUPERBELLS® CORALBERRY PUNCH
CALIBRACHOA

HABIT Mounding Trailing / *Mounding Trailing*
BLOOMS Planting to Hard Frost / *Plantar hasta la fuerte helada*
HEIGHT Short: 8–12"
Corto: 20–30cm
SPACING Min: 8" Max 12"
Mín: 20 cm Máx: 30 cm
ZONES Annual except in zones 9-11
Hardy to 30°F /
*Anual excepto en zonas 9-11
Resistente a 1°C*
FERTILIZE Regularly for best results /
Regularmente para obtener mejores resultados
WATER Normal / *Normal*
LIGHT Full to Part Sun
De Pleno a Medio Sol
FEATURES Heat Tolerant; Deadheading Not Necessary; Fall Interest / *Tolerante al calor; No es necesario retirar las hojas marchitas; Interés otoñal*
USES Containers / *Macetas*
CARE Easy / *Fácil*

www.provenwinners.com/fun

I'll be an *AFFAIR* to
REMEMBER.

THE BEST PLANTS TO TAKE HOME

The first rule of thumb is to start with quality plants. Top-quality plants may be a little more expensive, but they'll produce a much better display without time-consuming, troublesome fuss. For example, a six-pack of generic petunias seems like a bargain at the checkout counter, but they seldom have much vigor and will stop blooming unless you pinch off the spent flowers ("deadhead") routinely. Many petunias are likely to stop blooming anyway during summer heat and they must be cut back to control straggling growth. Proven Winners Supertunias, by contrast, have been bred to continue flowering without the need for deadheading, and they bloom profusely right through the dog days. Their growth is also naturally compact, and they are grown from cuttings guaranteed to be disease-free.

Make sure that any plants you intend to purchase are pest- and disease-free so you don't import these issues into your own landscape. Check the leaves—tops and bottoms—and along the stems for insects or insect eggs; discolored flecks or stickiness on the leaves may also be signs of insect infestation. Fungal or bacterial diseases can also hitchhike on the leaves and stems of plants—discolored spots or blotches on leaves are commonly signs of a problem.

For annual and perennial transplants, select compact plants with sturdy stems, crisp foliage, and which are not yet in full bloom. Avoid overly large transplants that have outgrown their containers. Likewise, avoid any plants with long roots emerging from the drainage holes in the bottoms of the pots. Such stressed plants have been left in the container too long and their future growth is likely to be disappointing. Container-grown shrubs are the easiest to transplant and the most readily available, but you can also purchase balled-and-burlapped (B&B) shrubs with root balls wrapped in burlap, or bare-root shrubs.

To check the health of a container-grown shrub, perennial, or annual, ask permission to remove the plant from its pot or cell pack. To do so, cover the top of the root ball with your hand, then gently turn the pot or pack upside down and give it a sharp tap on the bottom. The root ball will slide out so that you can see the condition of the roots. Roots should not be growing in a circle around the outside of the root ball; such plants should have been moved into a larger pot some time ago. Although it is possible to rehab these plants, they are not likely to perform well in your garden. Select plants with plenty of crisp, white young roots, but that are not root-bound (when the roots have taken up all the space in the container).

FERTILIZERS: WHAT KIND SHOULD I GET?

When shopping for plants, you'll likely also be shopping for fertilizer. The three numbers on the product label, such as 5-10-5 or 20-20-20, indicate the percentage by weight of the major nutrients—nitrogen (N), phosphorus (P), and potassium (K)—that the fertilizer contains.

Each of these three nutrients affects different parts of the plant. Nitrogen (the first number in the fertilizer formula) primarily fuels foliage growth. Phosphorus (the second number) promotes strong root growth and flower formation. Potassium (the third number) is essential to many of a plant's internal processes and so promotes strong growth; it also promotes cold hardiness and stress tolerance.

The balance of these nutrients within a fertilizer help determine its usefulness. Lawns, for example, because they are constantly replacing the leaf growth removed by mowing, respond well to fertilizers rich in nitrogen, which will be reflected in a high first number in the N-P-K ratio. Too much nitrogen, on the other hand, can promote leaf growth at the expense of flowering, so fertilizers designed for flowering plants are typically lower in the first number and higher in the succeeding two. Try to find a product labeled for the particular type of plant (turf, flowers, shrubs, etc.) you want to feed as each has particular needs and requires a different formulation.

▲ Fast-acting fertilizers like this plant food are best for annuals.

◄ This slow-acting fertilizer feeds plants for up to six months—perfect for shrubs and perennials.

Paying attention to the fertilizer formula will also help you get your money's worth. A 20-20-20 fertilizer may be somewhat more expensive than a 10-10-10 but because it's also twice as strong, it may be the better buy. In general, it's better to purchase a fertilizer labeled "complete" as it will contain all the major nutrients needed for plant growth. Ideally, your fertilizer should also contain the minor, trace, or "micro" elements that plants need in lesser quantities; these micro-elements are like vitamins, encouraging healthier growth.

In general, you should fertilize all plants at planting time. Shrubs and perennials respond best to a slow-acting fertilizer; fast-growing annuals benefit most from repeated doses of a fast-acting fertilizer.

- A slow-acting or timed-release fertilizer releases its nutrients slowly over time. Typically, this is the best choice for plants with a slower but sustained pattern of growth as with shrubs and perennials.

- A fast-acting fertilizer releases its nutrients immediately upon application and will give plants a quick boost. Such products, however, are not long-lasting. They are best reserved for fast-growing plants (annuals) because they may release more nutrients than slower-growing plants can use all at once, letting excess nutrients wash away. Such runaway nutrients are a waste of money and a common source of pollution in local waterways.

▲ This tropical-themed recipe includes papyrus plants, canna lilies, hibiscus, and lantanas.

FERTILIZERS FOR CONTAINERS VS. GARDEN BEDS

Frequent watering tends to wash the nutrients out of the potting mixes used in container plantings. In addition, many potting mixes contain no garden soil and so may be essentially nutrient-free. For this reason, it is important to get your containers on a regular schedule of fertilization right away. Choose a product specifically designed for potted plants and apply at the rate recommended on the product label. An N-P-K ratio, for example, of 16-8-12 offers an ideal balance of nutrients for potted plant growth: 16 percent nitrogen for enhanced leafy growth, 8 percent potassium for strong root growth and flowering, and 12 percent potash to promote cold hardiness and drought- and disease-resistance.

For in-ground gardens, test your soil before planting to determine what, if any, supplementary nutrients are needed (see page 42 for more about this). The test results clarify what fertilizers you should apply to nourish the type of plants you intend to grow. Don't forget that applying too much fertilizer can be as harmful as applying too little. Dry, granular fertilizers are much more likely to be used for in-ground plantings, although water-soluble fertilizers may be useful as a quick pick-me-up for annuals whose growth has stalled.

ORGANIC VS. SYNTHETIC FERTILIZERS

Many gardeners prefer to apply organic products exclusively, and they do have some advantages. Generally, organic fertilizers are slower to release their nutrients because they must first be broken down by microorganisms in the soil. This means that they feed your plants at a more gradual rate, one that is commonly better matched to the needs of the plants. Organic fertilizers also foster the microorganisms that are essential to healthy soil.

Organic fertilizers, however, are not as useful for feeding early spring plantings of cold-hardy annuals in the garden or in containers. That's because microorganisms are less active when the soil is still chilly. Indeed, organic fertilizers, even if applied early, are likely to simply sit in the garden bed or container until the weather and the soil warm. For this purpose, synthetic fertilizers, which don't need to be broken down by soil microorganisms, are superior.

Synthetic fertilizers are also, typically, more concentrated than organic fertilizers and so do not need to be applied in such large quantities. In addition, organic fertilizers may not be consistent in their strength. Animal manures, for example, a popular organic fertilizer, differ in their nutrient content depending on the diet of the animals that produced them.

From the Ground Up

A GUIDE TO
LANDSCAPE GARDENING

GETTING STARTED
WITH GARDENS

Nothing matches the color, lush beauty, and year-round appeal of a well-designed and well-planted bed of flowers and shrubs. If strategically placed, such a planting can dress up an entranceway, make a terrace ripe for outdoor entertaining, provide an inviting sanctuary, or transform a poolside sun deck. Such a bed can attract wildlife to your yard, fill the air with perfume, or brighten a winter day. You'll find all this and more in the following garden recipes.

WHEN TO PLANT YOUR GARDEN

Because climates vary with region, so does the appropriate time for planting a garden. For example, when spring begins in Dallas, Texas, or Phoenix, Arizona, winter is still in full force in Minneapolis, Minnesota. In frost-free climates, of course, you can plant at any time during the year, though you'll have to irrigate more faithfully should you choose to plant during a dry season.

However, where winter brings frost (USDA plant hardiness zones 1–9), it's best to wait until after the last spring frost to plant trees, shrubs, and perennial flowers. Ascertain the average date of the last spring frost in your area by consulting your state's cooperative extension service (see the resources). The staff at local garden centers and plant nurseries should also know the average date of the last spring frost and the beginning of planting season in your region. If all else fails, ask at the reference desk in your local public library.

◀ In a garden designed to attract butterflies, this Miss Molly butterfly bush is fulfilling its promise.

Gardeners commonly think of spring as the only planting season; however, for many types of plants, including hardy perennials and especially hardy trees and shrubs, fall is as good a time or better. Although air temperature cools with the arrival of fall, the soil remains relatively warm and perfect for planting well into the season. The warm soil is ideal for root growth, encouraging plantings to establish themselves in their new homes. You can enhance this effect by spreading mulch around fall plantings to insulate the soil's surface, helping it stay warm longer. Be sure to keep mulch a few inches away from the crown of any plant.

In fall, the cooler air temperatures result in less moisture loss from above-ground parts of plants. This translates into less post-planting stress. Furthermore, plants installed in fall have several extra months to recover from being transplanted before the stress of summer heat hits.

Another advantage of fall planting is that many plants are for sale at bargain prices then. Most garden centers are reluctant to store and maintain unsold plants over the winter and frequently mark them down to rock-bottom prices to encourage customers to take them off their hands. This makes fall an economical as well as horticulturally advantageous season for planting.

Hardy, cool-loving annuals, such as pansies, pansiolas, and lobelias, should be planted at the same time as shrubs and perennial flowers. But because Proven Winners grows its plants in containers, you can delay planting until later in the spring, if necessary. Annuals that require warm weather, such as marigolds, zinnias, and dahlias, should be planted *only* when daytime and nighttime temperatures remain at or above 60°F.

Where winters tend to be wet with frequent snow or rain, an additional consideration is the condition of your soil. Digging soil that is still muddy from the effect of such winter storms destroys its structure and makes it difficult for plants to grow roots. In such areas, it's important to wait until excess moisture has drained from the soil before planting. In general, it's always best to avoid stepping on planting areas and compacting the soil.

AMENDING YOUR SOIL

To foster strong plant growth, soil needs to be porous as well as nutrient rich. The best way to ensure both these qualities is to dig in plenty of organic material. Here are some types of organic matter to consider:

- Compost, whether purchased in bags or homemade from leaves, grass clippings, and kitchen scraps, is ideal, enhancing both porosity and fertility.

- Sphagnum peat (often called peat moss) will boost soil porosity but does not contribute any nutrients, so it will be necessary to add fertilizer as well.

- Dehydrated manure, sold in bags, is a significant source of nutrients but should be applied sparingly as it can be high in salts. When applied at the recommended rate, it is not sufficient to affect soil porosity.

- Composted bark also enhances soil porosity. Be sure to choose a product that is thoroughly decomposed; partially composted bark absorbs nutrients from the soil as it decomposes, creating a need to compensate with extra fertilization.

HOW MUCH?

The amount of organic matter you should add depends entirely on the soil's texture. The texture, in turn is a reflection of the proportions of the different mineral particles: sand, silt, and clay. Sand is the coarsest particle and feels abrasive; silt is finer and feels powdery when dry and slippery when wet; clay is the finest and feels greasy or sticky.

You can ascertain soil type or texture by having your soil professionally tested at your local cooperative extension (see the resources), or you can use the following do-it-yourself procedure. Dig a 2- to 3-inch deep hole in the proposed planting area, and grab a handful of soil. If the soil is dry, moisten it just slightly; then squeeze it into a ball. Drop this ball from waist height onto a hard surface. If the ball disintegrates on impact, you've got sandy soil; if the ball just cracks, your soil is predominantly clay; if the ball shatters into several pieces, you've got loam—soil with an ideal balance of sand, silt, and clay.

- *Sandy soil* needs extra irrigation and extra fertilization. Dig in 3–5 inches of organic matter—preferably compost—prior to planting to enhance fertility and the soil's ability to retain moisture. Re-treat annually thereafter (preferably after the plantings have gone dormant in fall) by sprinkling an inch of compost over the soil surface—remembering to keep the crowns of the plants uncovered.

- *Clay* is fertile but poorly drained. Improve porosity by digging in 3–5 inches of organic matter. The level of planting beds will be raised above that of surrounding soil to allow excess moisture to drain away and keep the soil from becoming water-logged.

- *Loam* is the ideal garden soil. Dig in 1–2 inches of organic matter before planting. Water and fertilize moderately.

STEPS FOR A NEW PLANTING

Thorough preparation is crucial to the success of any landscaping project. Getting the soil ready ahead of time and planning your design in advance ensures that the actual planting goes smoothly and quickly.

Each garden recipe includes the square footage needed for the design. Before you prepare the soil, mark the outline of your bed with stakes and string—this preview gives you a chance to check the scale of your planned planting. It may become apparent that the space you have marked out is too small or too large. You want it to be just right for the setting and at this point it is easy to make adjustments. A hose makes a useful tool for working out a curved outline. Arrange it into the perfect shape, then insert stakes at 2-foot intervals along its length and connect them with string.

Efficiency won't just save you time. Most plants are sold in pots and can only tolerate a limited period out of the ground without damage; a prolonged delay—a week or more—before planting will cause them to deteriorate and may stunt their growth permanently. Minimizing the time between bringing the plants home and getting them into the soil (and keeping them watered in the meantime) will markedly increase the success of your landscaping project.

PREPARING THE SOIL

Before you start to dig, check with your local utility company to determine if gas, electric, or water lines run through the targeted area. Then prepare the soil by following these steps.

1. Remove any turf and weeds from the intended planting area. Avoid injuring the roots of any existing bushes by digging only beyond the perimeter of their branches.

2. Spread the appropriate amount of organic matter over the proposed planting area. Sprinkle the area with the appropriate fertilizer.

3. With a spade or garden fork, dig soil to a depth of 8–12 inches, removing any rocks and major roots from nearby trees. A rototiller can perform this task, but hand digging is more thorough.

4. Rake the surface of the bed smooth and level.

Making Your Own Compost

You can buy the compost you need for your garden in bags or in bulk by the cubic yard, but it's also easy to make your own. Doing this also provides a convenient means of disposal for kitchen and garden debris. At its simplest, composting requires only stacking the debris in some inconspicuous spot, keeping it moist, and waiting for the natural processes of decay to do their work. Some points to observe include:

- Do not include any dairy products or meat scraps in your compost heap—these may attract rodents or other unwanted visitors.

- Don't overload the heap with green and wet materials, as this may cause the heap to develop an unpleasant odor. A good rule of thumb is to include 2 parts dry and brown materials (such as fallen leaves) to 1 part green and/or wet materials (such as kitchen scraps or fresh lawn clippings).

- During prolonged periods of dry weather, materials in the heap may dry out, which suspends their decay. If this happens, re-moisten the heap with a shower from the hose.

- Turning the materials in the heap occasionally with a garden fork helps aerate them and speed the decomposition process.

- Let the materials in the heap decompose completely into a dark brown or black crumbly material before adding them to the garden soil. The compost is ready when you can no longer distinguish the forms of any of the original ingredients. Adding immature compost to the garden can temporarily steal nutrients from the soil, thus starving your plants. One way to avoid this mistake is to start a new heap each year, and let the heaps from former years sit until they are fully decomposed before using them.

INTO THE GROUND

Now that the soil is ready, it's time to transfer your plants into the ground. If possible, plant on a cloudy day or at least in the late afternoon or evening to reduce water loss and stress.

1. Mark the spot where you plan to install each plant with a stake and lay out the plants beside the corresponding markers. If you are including container plantings as features of your new garden, set out the pots to check if these focal points will be in eye-pleasing spots.

2. Excavate a hole for each plant in the prepared soil as wide and deep as the plant's root ball.

3. Carefully remove the plants from their containers and with a knife or pointed stick gently tease out the soil from around the outer roots. If you encounter any circling roots, cut them with a sharp knife. Place the root ball in the prepared planting hole, holding the plant so that it is at the same level as it was in the container. Backfill around the roots with soil, pressing it in gently with your fingertips so that the plant won't fall over.

4. Water the newly installed plants, let the water soak in, and then water again to ensure that the soil around their roots is well moistened. In the case of larger plants such as shrubs and trees, it is helpful to surround them with a berm 2–3 inches high to help contain and infiltrate irrigation water.

MAINTENANCE AFTER PLANTING

Proven Winners plants are bred to require a minimum of care after planting. For example, a standard chore in most gardens is deadheading—the practice of pinching off aging flowers from annuals and perennials to enhance their appearance and, by keeping the plants from setting seed, to prolong their season of bloom. But many Proven Winners plants are sterile (they cannot set seed) and self-cleaning (the flowers fall off the plant naturally as they age). If you choose to include other plants in your garden, you should expect to spend a few minutes every few days pinching or snipping the fading blooms off your perennials and annuals. In general, it is neither necessary nor practical to deadhead shrubs.

No matter the quality of plant, one task you will have to confront is preventing weeds from over-running the garden after it is planted.

▶ Mulching between the colorful plants of this foliage-first garden helps keep weeds under control as well as keeping the soil moist, enhancing plant growth.

- **Compost:** Best if made from vegetable kitchen waste as composted garden waste may be a source of weed seeds; good source of plant nutrients but not very effective at weed suppression.

- **Cotton gin trash:** An economical choice in cotton-growing regions; useful source of plant nutrients.

- **Grass clippings:** Apply only when dried; do not use if grass has gone to seed or been treated with pesticides.

- **Pine or cedar bark nuggets or chips:** These come in different sizes; prone to washing away in heavy rain.

- **Pine fines:** Bark from pine trees, pieces too small for inclusion in bark mulch; also prone to washing away.

- **Pine needles:** Also called pine straw, this mulch is locally abundant in some regions of the South; economical, effective, and weed-free.

- **Rice, cocoa, and buckwheat hulls, and peanut shells:** May be economical in locations near processors; weed-free and effective.

- **Sawdust:** Best if composted before use; prone to blowing or washing away. Check the source before using to ensure that it doesn't include poison ivy.

- **Shredded hardwood bark:** If possible, check the source before using as it can be contaminated with poison ivy, or with black walnut and American beech barks, both of which suppress plant growth.

- **Shredded leaves:** Easily made at home in fall; economical and effective, more attractive when partially composted.

- **Spoiled hay:** An inexpensive option, but a source of weed seeds.

- **Straw:** Lightweight and readily available; may be contaminated with weed seeds.

CONTROLLING WEEDS

Controlling weeds starts when you are digging the garden, readying it for planting. At this point, take care to remove any weeds, especially perennial and deep-rooted ones, roots and all. This will help reduce your garden's weed population, but bear in mind that weed seeds are almost certainly lying dormant in the soil. When exposed to light by digging the bed, these are roused from dormancy. You can minimize the resulting weed growth by blanketing the soil between desirable plants with an organic mulch. If applied at planting time, the mulch will smother most germinating weed seeds. In addition, any new weed seeds that blow into the garden or that birds deposit will sit on the dry surface of the mulch where they are unlikely to germinate.

Many materials work well as an organic mulch. Availability will vary regionally, so a gardener in the South may find it more convenient to mulch with cotton gin trash or pine needles, while a Northeastern gardener is more likely to favor shredded autumn leaves.

Along with controlling weeds, organic mulch offers other benefits, such as keeping the soil moist by reducing water evaporation. A blanket of mulch also acts as insulation to help keep soil cool on hot days, which improves root growth of garden plants. (However, mulched soil does take longer to warm up in early spring.) As organic mulch decomposes, it adds humus to your soil, enhancing its structure and fertility.

You can also find garden weed preventers—products containing chemicals that inhibit weed germination and growth. These can be a great aid to controlling weeds in the garden, although the chemical weed inhibitors don't offer the additional benefits of mulch and may injure soil microorganisms that are important to plant growth. The effect of the chemical weed inhibitors is temporary, and typically you will have to reapply periodically over the course of the growing season.

An alternative, if temporary, aid to weed prevention, is landscape cloth. If spread over the surface of the soil before you plant—cut crossed slits into the cloth to install the plants—and then hidden with a layer of mulch it will help block the emergence of weeds for a couple of years. Over time, however, as the mulch decomposes, weeds will establish themselves over the cloth and even root into it. Pulling the weeds once they have rooted into the cloth is challenging and removing the failed landscape cloth is also laborious.

Whatever you employ as a weed-preventer, some of these invaders will undoubtedly defeat your defenses, popping up here and there through your mulch or in spite of your chemical treatments. Make a point of uprooting these weeds promptly. Weeds are easier to pull while the soil is moist and while they are still little, before their roots have penetrated deep into the soil. Above all, be sure to remove any weeds before they flower and scatter a new generation of weed seeds through your garden.

IRRIGATION

Irrigation is another necessity—your garden plants will need additional moisture during dry spells if they are to flourish. In arid and semi-arid regions such as the Southwest or the Rocky Mountain West, watering may be a necessity throughout the gardening season.

Let the plants tell you when they need water. Annual flowers are usually the first to show the effects of drought; leaf tips beginning to droop is a sign that the garden needs to be watered.

When you do water, apply the water slowly so that it doesn't run off across the surface of the ground, and make sure that it sinks deep into the soil. One easy way to test how deeply the water has penetrated is to push a rod or dowel down into the soil. It will pass easily through wet soil and stop when it reaches the dry soil below. Be sure to moisten the soil to a depth of 6–8 inches. Deep watering encourages the garden plants to send their roots down deep. This deeper penetration of the soil makes the plants better equipped to deal with drought. Frequent light watering, on the other hand, because it wets the soil only superficially, encourages shallow rooting and leaves plants more vulnerable to dry spells.

▲ Kits like this make installing drip irrigation easy.

Where water is in short supply, it is best to irrigate in the early morning when losses due to evaporation will be less. When watering, try not to wet the plant foliage as this encourages the spread of fungal diseases. Watering in the late afternoon means that plants will remain wet overnight—this not only promotes disease but it makes your garden more attractive to deer.

WATERING DEVICES

Many different devices are available for irrigating. A watering can offers a quick and easy way to water when you are irrigating just a couple of plants. Portable sprinklers, another common means of garden watering, offer flexibility but are relatively extravagant in their use of water. On dry, windy days as much as half of the water may evaporate before it reaches the soil. This is especially problematic in regions with saline water, where inefficient watering can damage plants by raising the salt content of the soil. In such regions, water only when necessary, water deeply when you do irrigate, and apply a mulch to keep water from evaporating off the soil surface, leaving its salts behind.

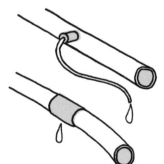

▲ Drip irrigation delivers water slowly, eliminating runoff, and targets plant roots precisely.

Drip irrigation systems or soaker hoses are far more efficient and healthy for your garden. Because they deposit the water right onto the soil in the region of the plants' roots, drip systems or soaker hoses commonly use half as much water as sprinklers to achieve the desired effect. This is an obvious advantage for gardeners in regions with limited water supplies, where water may be expensive. Because the plant foliage does not become wet, drip irrigation systems and soaker hoses are also less likely to foster plant diseases.

PRUNING

Pruning is another type of care essential to a flourishing garden. Typically Proven Winners plants are bred for compact growth, and thus require less pruning than similar generic plants. Still, selective trimming can be useful by allowing you to direct plant growth. Annuals, for example, often become bedraggled late in the growing season; cutting them back at that time by about one third forces out new growth that can restore a fresh appearance to the plants. Likewise, cutting back some perennials by one third as their flowers fade frequently sparks a second, although usually lesser, flush of bloom. In general, it is best to cut back to just above a leaf.

Careful pruning enhances the appearance and health of garden bushes. This is especially true of deciduous flowering shrubs, such as lilacs or roses. These bloom most prolifically on younger branches, so regular pruning to remove the oldest ones from the base will increase flowering.

One pruning a year is usually adequate. The best time of year to prune depends on the shrub's pattern of flowering. Some shrubs, including forsythia and azaleas, bloom from buds produced during the previous growing season; these are best pruned immediately after they flower. Other shrubs, such as Oso Easy roses, bloom from buds produced during the current season of growth; these are best pruned in early spring to encourage lots of new flower-bearing shoots.

If these instructions confuse you, just remember a basic rule of thumb. Prune spring-blooming shrubs immediately after they finish flowering; prune shrubs that bloom in summer or fall in early spring to prepare them for flowering on new growth later in the same year.

SHRUB PRUNING HOW-TO

Having decided when to prune, you next must determine how. A good rule is to start by removing the three Ds. That is, prune off any *dead* branches, any *damaged* branches, and any branches showing obvious signs of *disease*, such as withering leaves. When you remove a branch, use a sharp pair of pruning shears, loppers, or a pruning saw to cut off the branch at its base, or to cut it back to a healthy side branch.

After dealing with the three Ds, remove any ingrown branches (those growing back toward the interior of the shrub) at their bases. If you find crossing branches—pairs of branches rubbing against each other—remove the weaker branch, cutting it off at its base. In general, try to encourage open, outward-reaching growth to enable good air flow and a more attractive appearance.

Unless your intention is to turn a row of shrubs or trees into a formal hedge, a uniform wall of greenery, don't attack the plants with hedge trimmers. Shearing woody plants into spheres or cones destroys their structure, robbing them of their grace and natural beauty. This practice is also unhealthy for the plant: by removing all the foliage back to a single plane, you foster crowded growth that is an easy target for disease and an ideal hiding place for pests. If used at the wrong season, the hedge trimmers may also remove flower buds, reducing or eliminating altogether a shrub or tree's bloom.

◄ Early spring is the best time to prune summer-blooming shrubs like Oso Easy Paprika roses. These bloom from buds produced during the current season of growth, so this schedule of pruning encourages the development of new flower-bearing shoots.

Twelve Garden Recipes

◀ Prairie Winds Cheyenne Sky red switch grass and Tuscan Sun perennial
sunflowers are an attractive pairing in a songbird garden.

A Welcoming Entryway

TOTAL SPACE REQUIRED **230 square feet** • SITE **Full sun** • HARDINESS **Zones 6–8**

THE SCENE OUTSIDE the front door is what greets you as you arrive home at the end of the day; it's also what visitors see first. The entry to your home—whether cheerful or elegant or, alas, lackluster—creates expectations of what will be experienced inside. As the first view, the entryway garden also sets the tone for the landscape as a whole. A modest effort concentrated here can rejuvenate the entire front yard and in the process enhance your home's curb appeal. In this instance, the planting was disposed to enhance the effect of an existing Japanese maple (*Acer palmatum*).

WHEN TO PLANT Plant hollies, roses, coral bells, and autumn stonecrops after the average date of your last spring frost and when soil has drained sufficiently to be dug. Plant verbenas and summer snapdragons when daytime and nighttime temperatures remain at or above 60°F.

PEAK DISPLAY Continuous bloom from early summer (coral bells) through summer (roses, annual verbenas and summer snapdragons) and into fall (autumn stonecrops). The evergreen foliage of the Patti O hollies carries the display through winter.

Gardener's Hint

Oso Easy Petit Pink roses are "own root," which means they aren't grafted like conventional roses. Shrubs of this type are much longer lived.

INGREDIENTS

A **2 JAPANESE HOLLIES;** *Ilex crenata* PATTI O® (mature height 36–48 in., spread 12–24 in.)

B **4 ROSES;** *Rosa* OSO EASY® Petit Pink (mature height and spread 18–30 in.)

C **7 CORAL BELLS;** *Heuchera* PRIMO® Black Pearl (mature height 18–20 in., spread 26–30 in.)

SUBSTITUTIONS

North of zone 6, replace the Patti O hollies with Castle Spire blue hollies. They will produce bright red berries if a male pollinator such as Castle Wall is planted nearby.

Ilex ×meserveae CASTLE SPIRE®

Ilex ×meserveae CASTLE WALL®

D **6 AUTUMN STONECROPS;** *Sedum* ROCK 'N GROW® 'Maestro' (mature height 24–30 in., spread 24 in.)

E **19 VERBENAS;** *Verbena* SUPERBENA® Stormburst (mature height 6–12 in., spread 18–30 in.)

F **16 SUMMER SNAPDRAGONS;** *Angelonia* ANGELFACE® Super Blue (mature height 30–40 in., spread 12–18 in.)

DIRECTIONS

1. Plant the hollies on either side of path, 4–5 feet from the foundation, to anchor the planting.

2. Plant the roses in pairs on either side of the path in front of the hollies; allow each rose plant a space 30–42 in. across.

3. Arrange the perennial coral bells as color contrast around the base of the hollies; space them 26–30 inches apart.

4. Tuck in the autumn stonecrops, verbenas, and summer snapdragons around the outside of the planting, setting them out in clusters of two to five of each kind of plant. Space the stonecrop plants 20–24 inches apart, verbenas 8–12 inches apart, and snapdragons 10–14 inches apart.

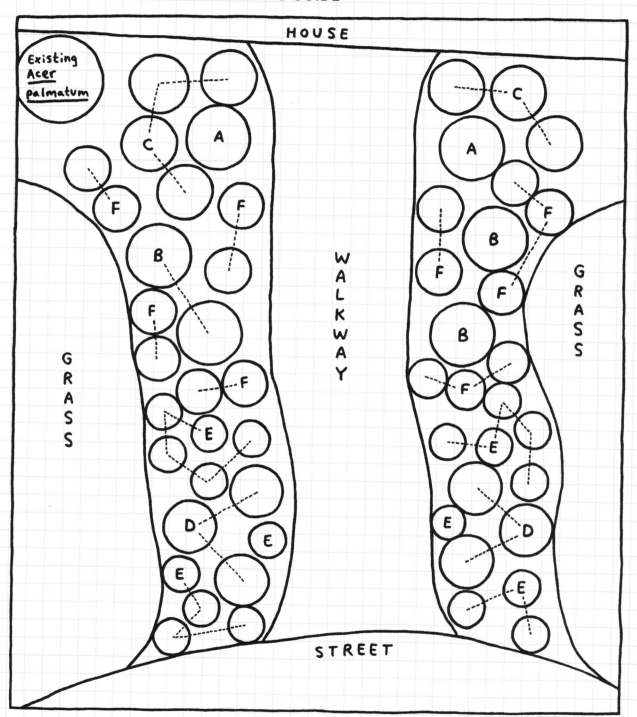

Songbird Garden

TOTAL SPACE REQUIRED **200 square feet** • SITE **Full sun** • HARDINESS **Zones 5–7**

FEATHERED VISITORS not only beautify the garden, filling it with color and song, but by feeding on insects they also help to protect it against pests, reducing the need for toxic pesticides. As a result, making your landscape a haven for songbirds is a win for you as well as for wildlife.

Providing the full smorgasbord of bird foods is an easy way to ensure a varied and rich songbird population. Berry-bearing shrubs such as viburnums and elderberries furnish an autumn feast for fruit-eaters so they can store up energy for the fall migration. Seed-eating birds will gravitate to the switch grass and perennial sunflowers, while the bee balm and large firecracker plants attract thirsty hummingbirds, as well as butterflies and native bees. Add a birdbath to complete the menu of attractions.

With these beautiful plants, you should be as happy as a lark in your songbird garden. Black Lace elderberry's elegant, finely cut, blackish-purple foliage makes a dramatic contrast to the pink parasols of flowers that the shrub bears in early summer; the red switch grass foliage provides a pleasing echo. The dark cherry pink flowers of the bee balm will delight your eyes, while the firecracker plant's floral explosions of red and yellow fully justify its name. The perennial sunflower provides a treasure of gold from midsummer through early fall. The final act in this drama is the clusters of pink and blue berries that the viburnum bears in fall.

WHEN TO PLANT Plant the viburnum, elderberry, red switch grasses, perennial sunflowers, and bee balms after the average date of your last spring frost and when soil has drained sufficiently to be dug. Plant the large firecracker plants and summer snapdragons when daytime and nighttime temperatures remain at or above 60°F.

PEAK DISPLAY The show starts with the counterpoint of white viburnum blossoms and blackish elderberry foliage in spring, continues with pink elderberry flowers in early summer, and golden sunflowers and cerise bee balm blossoms in midsummer to early fall, finishing with the colors of the viburnum berries and the wine-red autumn color of its foliage.

Gardener's Hint

Plant another variety of elderberry such as Black Beauty within 60 feet of your songbird garden to ensure cross-pollination and a larger crop of berries on Black Lace.

INGREDIENTS

A **1 VIBURNUM;** *Viburnum nudum* BRANDYWINE™ (mature height and spread 60–72 in.)

B **1 ELDERBERRY;** *Sambucus nigra* BLACK LACE® (mature height and spread 72–96 in.)

C **3 RED SWITCH GRASSES;** *Panicum virgatum* PRAIRIE WINDS® 'Cheyenne Sky' (mature height 30–36 in., spread 14–18 in.)

SUBSTITUTIONS

In zone 8 gardens substitute Pearl Glam beautyberry for the Black Lace elderberry.

Callicarpa PEARL GLAM®

DIRECTIONS

1. Locate the birdbath toward the end of the garden, setting it far enough forward that it won't be hidden by the plants.

2. First plant the shrubs—the viburnum and the elderberry— to provide structure around which to build the rest of the planting. Allow the viburnum a space 6 feet across; allow the elderberry 7 feet.

3. Arrange the switch grasses between the shrubs and toward the back of the garden, allowing a space of 14–18 inches for each.

4. Distribute the perennial sunflowers and firecracker plants in front of the shrubs and switch grasses. Allow each sunflower a planting space 20–24 inches across and each firecracker plant a space 12–18 inches across.

5. Tuck in the bee balms around the front of the garden, and the summer snapdragons near the birdbath. Allow each bee balm a space 10–12 inches across, and each summer snapdragon a space 12–14 inches across.

D 6 PERENNIAL SUNFLOWERS; *Heliopsis helianthoides* 'Tuscan Sun' (mature height and spread 20–24 in.)

E 3 LARGE FIRECRACKER PLANTS; *Cuphea* VERMILLIONAIRE® (mature height 18–28 in., spread 12–24 in.)

F 6 BEE BALMS; *Monarda didyma* 'Pardon My Cerise' (mature height 14–18 in., spread 10–12 in.)

G 6 SUMMER SNAPDRAGONS; *Angelonia angustifolia* ANGELFACE® White (mature height 18–24 in., spread 12–18 in.)

PLANTING GUIDE

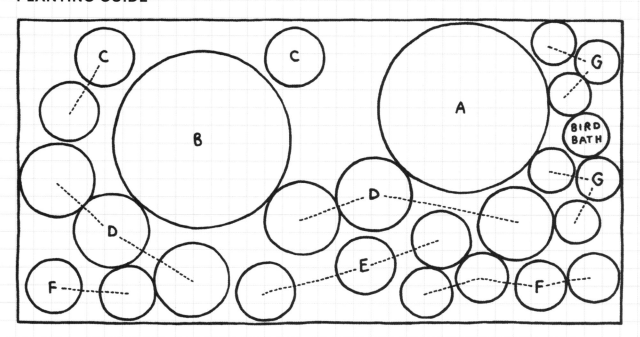

Butterfly and Pollinator Garden

TOTAL SPACE REQUIRED **150 square feet** • SITE **Full sun** • HARDINESS **Zones 5–9**

WE DEPEND ON BUTTERFLIES and other pollinators to fertilize flowers and make possible the production of our vegetables and fruits, as well as the seeds for our garden flowers. Yet these beneficial insects are declining in number, largely because of a loss of habitat. With this garden, you can do your part to reverse that trend, and at the same time fill your landscape with fluttering, jewel-like colors. Who could refuse that combination?

What's more, this garden will furnish an eye- and nose-pleasing assortment of flowers all summer long. They will even draw hummingbirds, another welcome bonus. All in all, you're likely to find yourself enjoying this plot as much as the butterflies do.

WHEN TO PLANT Plant butterfly bushes and autumn stonecrops after the average date of your last spring frost and when soil has drained sufficiently to be dug. Plant salvias, lantanas, flossflower, bidens, and catmint when daytime and nighttime temperatures remain at or above 60°F.

PEAK DISPLAY The annuals (lantanas and salvias) will bloom from spring to frost; the butterfly bush (a non-invasive hybrid) blooms from midsummer to late fall; and the autumn stonecrop (perennial in zones 3–9) blooms, as its name suggests, in early fall.

Gardener's Hint

For the greatest benefit to the butterflies, grow plants that the caterpillars use for food alongside this garden. For instance, the monarch butterflies that your flowers attract are likely to lay eggs and start a new generation if you grow milkweeds nearby. Also provide a mud puddle where butterflies and moths can obtain salts and minerals absent from their diet of nectar. All you need is a shallow dish filled with gravel and mud; keep it watered if there is no rain.

INGREDIENTS

A **3 BUTTERFLY BUSHES;** *Buddleia* 'Miss Molly' (mature height and spread 48–60 in.)

B **6 SALVIAS;** *Salvia splendens* purple cultivar (mature height 18–26 in., spread 12–18 in.)

C **2 AUTUMN STONECROPS;** *Sedum* ROCK 'N GROW® 'Lemonjade' (mature height 16–18 in., spread 26–28 in.)

SUBSTITUTIONS

Those who favor native plants may replace the butterfly bushes with Vanilla Spice summersweet shrubs, which reach a mature height of 3–6 feet. The purple salvias can be swapped out with Color Spires Indiglo Girl salvias.

Salvia COLOR SPIRES® Indiglo Girl

Clethra alnifolia VANILLA SPICE®

DIRECTIONS

1. Locate (here along a fence) and plant the butterfly bushes first as focal points around which you will build the garden. Allow each shrub a space 5–6 feet across.

2. Intermingle the salvias and autumn stonecrops in front of the butterfly bushes. Allow each salvia a space 12–18 inches across, and each autumn stonecrop 26–28 inches across.

3. Accent the salvias and stonecrops with spots of catmint, flossflower, and bidens.

4. Plant the lantanas as a broad edging in the front of the garden. Each lantana needs a space 20–24 inches across.

D **1 CATMINT;** *Nepeta faassenii* 'Cat's Meow' (mature height 17–20 in., spread 12–18 in.)

E **1 FLOSSFLOWER;** *Ageratum* ARTIST® Purple (mature height 8–12 in., spread 6–10 in.)

F **3 BIDENS;** *Bidens ferulifolia* GOLDILOCKS ROCKS® (mature height 12–14 in., spread 14–18 in.)

G **8 LANTANAS;** *Lantana camara* LUSCIOUS® Lemonade (mature height 24–36 in., spread 20–24 in.)

PLANTING GUIDE

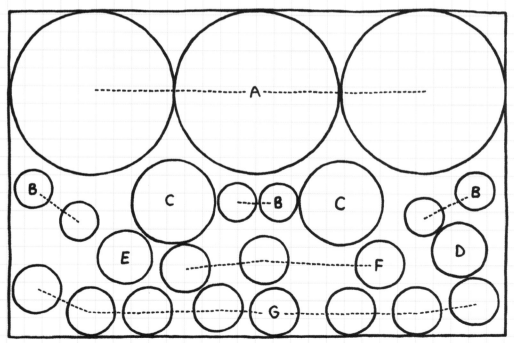

Evening Garden for Entertaining

TOTAL SPACE REQUIRED **180 square feet** • SITE **Full sun to part shade** • HARDINESS **Zones 3–9**

THE PLANTING THAT SPARKLES in the midday sun dims with the sunset; to captivate your evening guests you need a different color palette. Reds, blues, and other intense colors disappear as darkness falls, while paler shades, especially whites, take on a glow in the twilight and the gentler illumination of outdoor lighting. Flowers that might appear washed out at noon become beacons in the evening landscape, and petunias, which release their perfume as night falls, lend this garden a special romance.

WHEN TO PLANT Plant the smooth hydrangea after the average date of your last spring frost and when soil has drained sufficiently to be dug. Plant the sweet alyssum and petunias when daytime and nighttime temperatures remain at or above 60°F.

PEAK DISPLAY Late spring through mid-fall, when the hydrangea blossoms age to pink, red, and burgundy.

Gardener's Hint

Incrediball hydrangeas bloom only on the current season's growth, so any pruning should be done in late winter or very early spring; pruning later in the season will diminish the floral display.

DIRECTIONS

1. Plant the smooth hydrangea near an outdoor entertaining spot, such as the edge of a patio or deck. Allow the shrub a space at least 5 feet across.

2. Set out the sweet alyssum and petunias around and in front of the hydrangea; plant sweet alyssum 18–24 inches apart and petunias 12–18 inches apart.

INGREDIENTS

A **1 SMOOTH HYDRANGEA;** *Hydrangea arborescens*
INCREDIBALL® (mature height and spread 48–60 in.)

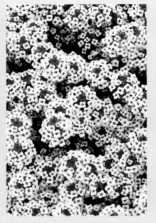

B **8 SWEET ALYSSUM;**
Lobularia SNOW PRINCESS®
(mature height 4–8 in.,
spread 24–48 in.)

C **8 PETUNIAS;** *Petunia*
SUPERTUNIA® White
(mature height 6–12 in.,
spread 18–24 in.)

SUBSTITUTIONS

If your space is too
small to accommodate
Incrediball hydrangeas
substitute Invincibelle
Wee White, a smooth
hydrangea which won't
exceed a mature height
of 30 inches.

INVINCIBELLE WEE WHITE®

PLANTING GUIDE

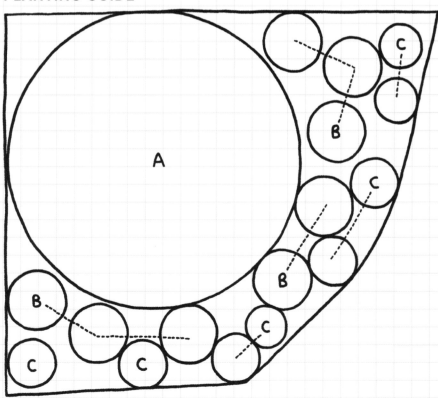

Seaside Garden

TOTAL SPACE REQUIRED **300 square feet** • SITE **Full sun** • HARDINESS **Zones 5–9**

Gardener's Hint

Sandy soils do not retain moisture well; when planting your seaside garden, dig in plenty of compost or other organic material and irrigate at least weekly during rainless periods through the first growing season.

Time at the beach may be a vacation for you and your family, but it's a tough trial for most garden plants. Drought-prone sandy soils, winds filled with salt spray, and unrelenting sunshine make this habitat challenging. Fortunately, a select group of plants is able to cope. We've outlined how to combine a number of these into a pleasing garden that will enhance any holiday cottage.

Gardeners who don't live near the coast but whose landscape features sandy soils or frequent drought, exposure to full sun, and saline water (a common combination in the Southwest) may also find inspiration in this design. Wherever you plant it, this combination of colorful flowers and handsome foliages is sure to please.

WHEN TO PLANT Plant summersweet, hydrangeas, roses, and switch grasses after the average date of your last spring frost and when soil has drained sufficiently to be dug. Plant lavenders, verbenas, dwarf morning glories, gerbera daisies, African daisies, and strawflowers when daytime and nighttime temperatures remain at or above 60°F.

PEAK DISPLAY The backbone of the floral display is the annuals—verbenas, dwarf morning glories, gerbera daisies, African daisies, and strawflowers—that bloom from planting until frost. The hydrangeas bloom and rebloom all summer long (unlike the traditional types that only bloom once), as do the lavenders. Midsummer brings the summersweet, whose jumbo white flower clusters are sweetly fragrant, and the roses, which continue to bloom through early fall.

INGREDIENTS

A **1 SUMMERSWEET;** *Clethra alnifolia* VANILLA SPICE®
(mature height 36–72 in., spread 36–60 in.)

B **2 HYDRANGEAS;**
Hydrangea macrophylla
LET'S DANCE® BLUE
JANGLES® (mature height
12–24 in., spread 24–36 in.)

C **3 ROSES;** *Rosa* OSO
EASY® Paprika (mature
height 12–24 in., spread
24–36 in.)

D **4 SWITCH GRASSES;** *Panicum virgatum* PRAIRIE
WINDS® 'Apache Rose' (mature height 40–48 in.,
spread 26–30 in.)

E **3 LAVENDERS;**
Lavandula angustifolia
SWEET ROMANCE®
(mature height and
spread 12–18 in.)

F **3 VERBENAS;**
Verbena bonariensis
METEOR SHOWER®
(mature height 20–30 in.,
spread 8–12 in.)

(continued next page)

INGREDIENTS, *continued*

G **8 DWARF MORNING GLORIES;** *Evolvulus* BLUE MY MIND® (mature height 6–12 in. spread 12–24 in.)

H **8 GERBERA DAISIES;** *Gerbera* orange cultivar (mature height 12–20 in., spread 10–14 in.)

I **6 AFRICAN DAISIES;** *Osteospermum* BRIGHT LIGHTS™ Yellow (mature height and spread 8–12 in.)

J **8 STRAWFLOWERS;** *Chrysocephalum apiculatum* FLAMBE® Yellow (mature height and spread 8–14 in.)

DIRECTIONS

1. Site and plant the shrubs—the summersweet, hydrangeas, and roses—first to establish a structure and backdrop around which you can arrange the perennials and annuals. Allow the summersweet a space of 5–6 feet, the hydrangeas 24–36 inches each, and the roses 36–48 inches each.

2. Arrange the perennial plants—switch grasses and lavenders—around the shrubs. Allow each switch grass a space of 26–30 inches, and the lavenders a space of 12–18 inches each.

3. Lay out groups of the annuals—verbenas, dwarf morning glories, gerbera daisies, African daisies, and strawflowers—around the periphery so that they will be easy to replace each spring. Allow the verbenas a space of 8–12 inches each, the dwarf morning glories 8–12 inches each, the gerbera daisies 10–12 inches each, the African daisies 6–10 inches each, and the strawflowers 8–12 inches each.

SUBSTITUTIONS

For a more floriferous look, replace the summersweet with a Ruby Anniversary abelia, and the lavenders with Angelface Wedgwood Blue summer snapdragons. Or add greater warmth to the palette by replacing the 'Apache Rose' switch grasses with an equal number of the red-leaved switch grass 'Cheyenne Sky'.

Abelia chinensis
RUBY ANNIVERSARY®

Angelonia ANGELFACE®
Wedgwood Blue

Panicum virgatum PRAIRIE
WINDS® 'Cheyenne Sky'

PLANTING GUIDE

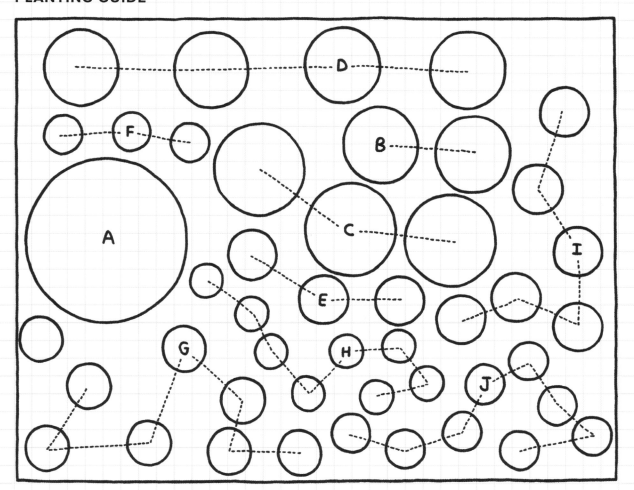

Fragrant Flower Garden

TOTAL SPACE REQUIRED **132 square feet** • SITE **Full sun** • HARDINESS **Zones 4–7**

A GARDEN SHOULD DELIGHT not just the eye but the nose as well. This one is designed to do both, offering a parade of colorful flowers as well as a succession of perfumes. Here, the garden recipe has been combined with an existing planting of two Fluffy western arborvitaes, which help provide structure and color.

The sweet, old-fashioned scent of lilac fills the spring air, then re-emerges from midsummer into fall as these compact shrubs bloom again. Fast-growing Supertunia 'Bordeaux' petunias exhale their fragrance in summer evenings; late in the season they are joined by the heady perfumes of blush-colored phlox and violet-blossomed clematis. The silver foliage of Russian sage makes not just an admirable setting for its blue flowers, but also furnishes a clean, aromatic scent that serves as a season-long background note for the sweeter floral fragrances.

If possible, locate this garden near a sitting area so that you can savor it at leisure. You may find that it takes you straight back to childhood afternoons in your grandmother's garden—remembered fragrances have a remarkable power to call up memories.

WHEN TO PLANT Plant the sweet autumn clematis, lilacs, Russian sages, and phloxes after the average date of your last spring frost and when soil has drained sufficiently to be dug. Plant the petunias when daytime and nighttime temperatures remain at or above 60°F.

PEAK DISPLAY Flowers from spring to fall, fragrant foliage throughout the growing season.

> *Gardener's Hint*
>
> **Renew the perennials (Russian sage and phlox) by cutting them back to a height of a few inches just before growth resumes in spring. Prune sweet autumn clematis at the same time, cutting all stems back to a strong bud about 12 inches from the ground.**

INGREDIENTS

A **1 SWEET AUTUMN CLEMATIS;** *Clematis* 'Sweet Summer Love' (mature height 120–180 in., spread 72–120 in.)

B **3 LILACS;** *Syringa* BLOOMERANG® Dwarf Pink (mature height and spread 30–36 in.)

SUBSTITUTIONS

In gardens south of zone 7, replace the lilacs with an equal number of Sweet Emotion fragrant abelias.

Abelia mosanensis
SWEET EMOTION®

DIRECTIONS

1. Locate and plant the sweet autumn clematis to serve as the focal point of the garden.

2. Plant the lilacs around the front of autumn clematis, spacing them 4 feet apart and 4 feet from the clematis.

3. Plant the Russian sages in front of the lilacs, setting them about 3 feet apart and 3–3.5 feet from the bases of the lilacs.

4. Plant the phloxes on either side of the garden, locating them at least 2.5 feet from the base of the lilacs, and 2 feet from the base of the Russian sages.

5. Tuck the petunias among and in front of the perennials and shrubs to provide color during the first season. The need for these annuals will decrease in future years as the perennials and shrubs mature and expand to fill the garden.

C **3 RUSSIAN SAGES;** *Perovskia atriplicifolia* 'Denim 'N Lace' (mature height 28–32 in., spread 34–38 in.)

D **2 PHLOXES;** *Phlox paniculata* 'Opening Act Blush' (mature height and spread 18–20 in.)

E **24 PETUNIAS;** *Petunia* SUPERTUNIA® Bordeaux™ (mature height 6–12 in., spread 18–24 in.)

PLANTING GUIDE

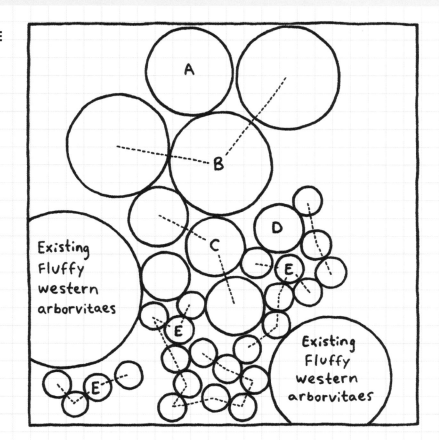

Existing Fluffy western arborvitaes

Existing Fluffy western arborvitaes

A
B
C
D
E
E
E

Shady Summertime Retreat

TOTAL SPACE REQUIRED **100 square feet** • SITE **Part shade to shade** • HARDINESS **Zones 3–9**

BY THE TIME the dog days of summer settle in, the sunny parts of the garden are out of bounds, too hot to enjoy for most of the day. That's when you appreciate a garden nestled among trees, a place where you can enjoy the shade while sipping a cooling drink, and, of course, admire the flowers. The planting illustrated here takes advantage of the shade provided by the garden's established cornelian cherry tree (*Cornus mas*).

Finding flowers that can tolerate both shade and summer heat is a challenge, but we have identified three (browallias, New Guinea impatiens, and wishbone flowers) that will fill your shady retreat with color. For contrast we've also included two spectacular foliage plants. The stunning leaves of Shadowland 'Empress Wu' hosta may reach 28 inches long and 25 inches wide, and when mature in several years, the plant will form a mound up to 4 feet tall and 6 feet wide. Though lush foliage is the main attraction of this hosta, it also flowers, sending up stalks of purple blossoms in early to midsummer, just when you'll be most drawn to your retreat. The Kodiak Orange bush honeysuckle contributes another foliar note, emerging with orange leaves that turn to a glowing orange in fall.

WHEN TO PLANT Plant the hostas and bush honeysuckle after the average date of your last spring frost and when soil has drained sufficiently to be dug. Plant the New Guinea impatiens, wishbone flowers, and browallias when daytime and nighttime temperatures remain at or above 60°F.

PEAK DISPLAY The annuals (New Guinea impatiens, wishbone flowers, and browallias) will bloom from planting time until the first fall frost, but make their greatest show in summertime, when they will be joined in bloom by the hosta. The bush honeysuckle bears clusters of pale yellow flowers throughout the summer and shines with bright orange foliage in the fall, making it a native substitute for the invasive burning bush (*Euonymus alatus*).

Gardener's Hint

For the best bloom, irrigate these flowers whenever the leaves show signs of flagging. Treat with a water-soluble fertilizer once a month during late spring and summer.

INGREDIENTS

A **6 HOSTAS;** *Hosta* SHADOWLAND® 'Empress Wu' (mature height 44–48 in., spread 60–72 in.)

B **1 BUSH HONEYSUCKLE;** *Diervilla* KODIAK® Orange (mature height and spread 36–48 in.)

SUBSTITUTIONS

For smaller properties, economize on space by replacing Shadowland 'Empress Wu' with Shadowland 'Wheee!', a more compact hosta with ruffled, golden-edged leaves that make a lively background for this garden's blossoms.

Hosta SHADOWLAND® 'Wheee!'

DIRECTIONS

1. Set the bench at the center of a shaded area.

2. Distribute and plant the hostas and the bush honeysuckle around the back periphery of your shady retreat, to serve as a framework into which to insert the annual flowers. Allow the bush honeysuckle a space 3 feet across; set the hostas 4 feet apart.

3. Plant the New Guinea impatiens in two clusters of four, flanking and emphasizing the bench. Set the impatiens 6–8 inches apart.

4. Distribute the wishbone flowers and browallias in masses to create strong splashes of color. Set the browallias and wishbone flowers 10 inches apart.

C **8 NEW GUINEA IMPATIENS;** *Impatiens hawkeri* INFINITY® Blushing Lilac (mature height 10–14 in., 6–12 in.)

D **6 WISHBONE FLOWERS;** *Torenia* CATALINA® Midnight Blue (mature height 8–16 in., spread 8–10 in.)

E **7 BROWALLIAS;** *Browallia* ENDLESS™ Flirtation (mature height 12–16 in., spread 10–14 in.)

PLANTING GUIDE

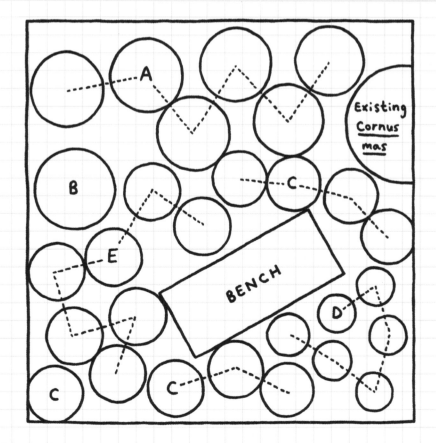

Existing Cornus mas

BENCH

Hot and Sunny Garden

TOTAL SPACE REQUIRED **210 square feet** • SITE **Full sun** • HARDINESS **Zones 3–8**

A HOT AND SUNNY GARDEN is both an opportunity and a challenge. The bright, day-long sunshine that falls on the south side of a house or fence, or a south-facing slope, can fuel impressive plant growth and generate bumper crops of flowers. But the hot, dry environment demands especially tough plants; ordinary garden plants are likely to wither in such a setting. Provided adequate care, the robust plants that fill this garden will relish the extra heat and sun, rewarding you with dazzling, season-long bloom.

Give a bit of extra attention to preparing the soil for this garden, digging in a couple of inches of compost or sphagnum peat so that it will absorb and retain water more easily. When you finish planting, lay down soaker hoses so that you can deliver water right to the bases of the plants, thus minimizing water lost to evaporation. Then cover the surface of the garden with a couple of inches of loose, organic mulch such as shredded bark or pine needles—this will help conserve moisture while keeping the soil cooler.

WHEN TO PLANT Plant the panicle hydrangea and perennial sunflowers after the average date of your last spring frost and when soil has drained sufficiently to be dug. Plant the dahlias, salvias, bidens, and petunias when daytime and nighttime temperatures remain at or above 60°F.

PEAK DISPLAY Annual bidens and petunias begin blooming in late spring, with the salvias (perennial from zone 7 southward), dahlias (perennial from zone 8 south), and perennial sunflowers (hardy from zone 3–9) chiming in by early summer. In late summer the panicle hydrangea (hardy from zone 3–8) provides a finale of greenish 6- to 8-inch flower clusters that turn a rich pink and hang on well into fall.

Gardener's Hint

This garden's robust growth and profuse flowering demands extra attention to fertilization. Be sure to apply slow-release fertilizer in early spring; if you live where the growing season is long, apply again after six months.

INGREDIENTS

A **1 PANICLE HYDRANGEA;** *Hydrangea paniculata* 'Limelight' (mature height and spread 72–96 in.)

B **6 PERENNIAL SUNFLOWERS;** *Heliopsis helianthoides* 'Tuscan Sun' (mature height and spread 20–24 in.)

C **7 DAHLIAS;** *Dahlia* Mystic Illusion (mature height 18–36 in., spread 12–16 in.)

SUBSTITUTIONS

If you can't locate the salvia, use 'Cat's Meow' catmint instead. If the bidens are unavailable, use an equal number of Golddust mecardonias.

Nepeta faassenii 'Cat's Meow'

Mecardonia **GOLDDUST®**

DIRECTIONS

1. Plant the panicle hydrangea first to anchor the back of the design; set it 6 feet apart from other plants as it is a vigorous grower.

2. Plant the perennial sunflowers around the hydrangea, allowing each plant a space 18 inches across.

3. Intermingle the dahlias and salvias around and in front of the perennial sunflowers, allowing each dahlia a space 12–16 inches across and the salvias 14–18 inches across.

4. Plant the mecardonias in two clusters in front of the salvias, allowing each plant a space 12–16 inches across.

5. Tuck in the petunias around the outer edge of the garden, allowing each plant a space 12–18 inches across.

D **6 SALVIAS;** *Salvia longispicata*
×*farinacea* ROCKIN'® PLAYIN' THE BLUES®
(mature height 24–48 in., spread
24–36 in.)

E **12 BIDENS;** *Bidens ferulifolia*
GOLDILOCKS ROCKS® (mature height
12–14 in., spread 14–18 in.)

F **7 PETUNIAS;** *Petunia*
SUPERTUNIA VISTA® Fuchsia
(mature height 12–24 in.,
spread 24–36 in.)

PLANTING GUIDE

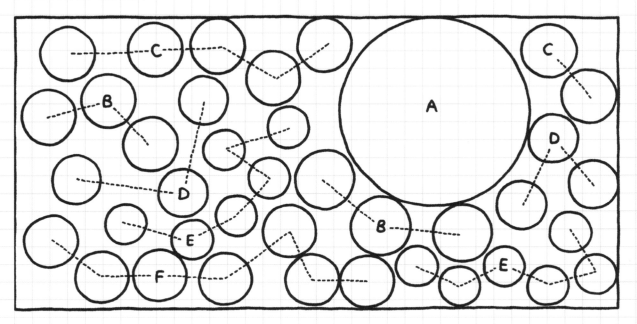

Colorful Foliage Garden

TOTAL SPACE REQUIRED **64 square feet** • SITE **Full sun to part shade** • HARDINESS **Zones 4–8**

IN OUR ENTHUSIASM FOR FLOWERS, gardeners often overlook the beauty that foliage can bring to the landscape. After all, flowers are spectacular but fleeting; the leaves give a plant its day-in, day-out character from budbreak in spring to autumn's fall, and even beyond in the case of evergreens such as the foamy bells. In this planting, the foliage holds center stage, and the flowers—for these plants do bloom—are a welcome bonus.

One trick this garden employs effectively is highlighting a pair of colorful plants by elevating them in a garden urn. (This urn used in this recipe is 16 inches across × 21.5 inches tall, with an 18-inch planting depth). Because of their modest stature, the red switch grass and foamy bells might otherwise be lost in this planting, but putting them on a pedestal ensures that they play a starring role. The variegated white-and-green foliage of the weigela provides a refreshing contrast to the shrub's pink flowers.

WHEN TO PLANT Plant the fountain grasses, coral bells, weigelas, red switch grass, and foamy bells after the average date of your last spring frost and when soil has drained sufficiently to be dug.

PEAK DISPLAY Spring through fall, with evergreen notes supplied by the foliage of the foamy bells and coral bells.

Gardener's Hint

The naturally compact size of My Monet weigela means that you won't need to prune this shrub.

INGREDIENTS
In urn

A **1 RED SWITCH GRASS;** *Panicum virgatum* PRAIRIE WINDS® 'Cheyenne Sky' (mature height 30–36 in., spread 14–18 in.)

B **6 FOAMY BELLS;** *Heucherella* FUN AND GAMES® 'Red Rover' (mature height 28–34 in., spread 18–20 in.)

SUBSTITUTIONS

To introduce a lighter color scheme, replace the urn's switch grass with Graceful Grasses King Tut Egyptian papyrus surrounded with Lemon Coral Mexican stonecrops instead of the foamy bells. Retain the fountain grass around the urn, but replace the coral bells with Fun and Games 'Leapfrog' foamy bells, and change up the weigela with Crème Fraiche deutzia.

Cyperus papyrus GRACEFUL GRASSES® KING TUT®

Sedum mexicanum LEMON CORAL™

Deutzia gracilis CRÈME FRAICHE®

Heucherella FUN AND GAMES® 'Leapfrog'

In ground

C **2 WEIGELAS;** *Weigela florida* MY MONET® (mature height 12–18 in., spread 18–24 in.)

D **6 CORAL BELLS;** *Heuchera* PRIMO® 'Black Pearl' (mature height 18–20 in., spread 26–30)

E **4 FOUNTAIN GRASSES;** *Pennisetum setaceum* GRACEFUL GRASSES® 'Sky Rocket' (mature height 24–30 in., spread 16–20 in.)

DIRECTIONS

1. Place the urn to serve as the focal point of the display and fill with potting mix. Plant the switch grass at its center and surround with foamy bells.

2. Arrange the weigelas at the foot of and in front of urn. Allow each weigela a space 24–30 inches across.

3. Flank the weigelas with coral bells, three on each side, allowing each plant a space 26–30 inches across.

4. Back the urn with a semicircle of fountain grasses, allowing each grass a planting spot 16–20 inches across.

PLANTING GUIDE

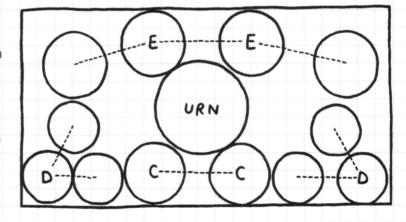

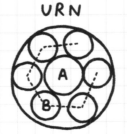

Bold Tropical Effects

TOTAL SPACE REQUIRED **120 square feet** • SITE **Full sun** • HARDINESS **Zones 9–11**

Gardener's Hint

The cannas and dahlias aren't winter-hardy north of zone 8. For a repeat performance the following year dig the roots from the ground after fall's first frost and store over the winter in a cool basement in a box of barely damp sphagnum peat. If you have a warm, bright sun porch, you can overwinter the papyruses as potted houseplants, and then move them back to the garden after the danger of frost is past the following spring.

WHO HASN'T EVER WANTED to escape to a tropical paradise? With this garden you can enjoy your getaway without leaving your backyard. Brilliant blossoms and flamboyant foliage combine in a luxurious display that can turn a corner of a patio or terrace into a South Pacific hideaway. Add a couple of Tiki torches and you are ready for summertime entertaining.

On a practical note, this garden is especially suited to climates that, while their winters may be chilly, have hot and humid summers. Such summer weather may be challenging for many hardy plants, but the tropical transplants featured here will relish it and respond by growing like weeds.

WHEN TO PLANT Plant the papyruses, canna lilies, rose mallow, lantanas, dahlias, gerbera daisies, and sweet potato vines when daytime and nighttime temperatures remain at or above 60°F.

PEAK DISPLAY From midsummer into early fall in the North; late spring to mid fall in the South.

INGREDIENTS

A **3 EGYPTIAN PAPYRUSES;** *Cyperus papyrus* GRACEFUL GRASSES® KING TUT® (mature height 48–72 in., spread 36–48 in.)

B **5 CANNA LILIES;** *Canna generalis* TOUCAN® Rose (mature height 30–48 in., spread 18–24 in.)

C **1 ROSE MALLOW;** *Hibiscus* SUMMERIFIC® 'Cherry Choco Latte' (mature height and spread 44–48 in.)

SUBSTITUTIONS

For a part sun situation, replace this recipe's sun-loving flowers (gerbera daisies, dahlias, and lantanas) with shade-tolerant tropical foliage plants such as Artful Heartfire angel wings, Royal Hawaiian Hawaiian Punch elephant's ear, and Infinity Red New Guinea impatiens.

Colocasia esculenta ROYAL HAWAIIAN® Hawaiian Punch

Caladium hortulanum ARTFUL® HEARTFIRE®

Impatiens hawkeri INFINITY® Red

DIRECTIONS

1. Begin by arranging the taller plants—papyruses, canna lilies, and rose mallow—at the back of the planting area. Space papyrus plants 3–4 feet apart, cannas 1.5–2 feet apart, and rose mallow 4–5 feet apart.

2. Group the lantanas in front and to the side of the papyrus plants and cannas, allowing each plant a space of 18–24 inches across.

3. Arrange the dahlias and gerbera daisies in front, spacing dahlias 12–16 inches apart and gerbera daisies 10–12 inches apart.

4. Edge with sweet potato vines, allowing each plant a space 10–12 inches across.

D 6 LANTANAS;
Lantana camara
LUSCIOUS® BANANARAMA™
(mature height 18–30 in.,
spread 18–36 in.)

E 3 DAHLIAS; *Dahlia
variabilis* DAHLIGHTFUL®
Georgia Peach (mature
height 20–30 in., spread
20–24 in.)

F 7 GERBERA DAISIES;
Gerbera magenta cultivar
(mature height 12–20 in.,
spread 12–14 in.)

G 3 SWEET POTATO
VINES; *Ipomoea batatas*
ILLUSION® Emerald Lace
(mature height 6–10 in.,
spread 24–36 in.)

PLANTING GUIDE

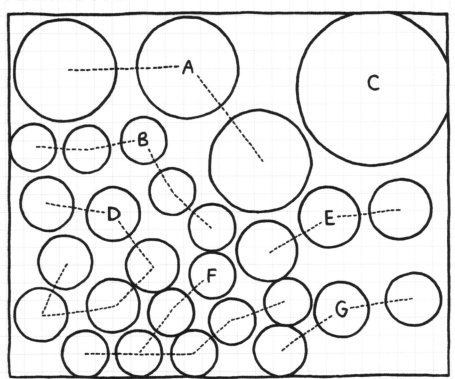

Spring and Fall Garden

TOTAL SPACE REQUIRED **180 square feet** • SITE **Full sun** • HARDINESS **Zones 4–8**

DO YOU TRAVEL during the summer? Perhaps you are away in a cabin in the mountains or a cottage on the shore. Why not plan a garden that fits your schedule, looking its best when you're home to enjoy it?

This garden is designed to provide flowers during the summer—yes, you *can* have it all—but is most vibrant during the spring and fall. It will thrive in any well-drained sunny spot with average soil, and offers a combination of vivid foliage and bright blossoms through spring and again in fall, when you have returned from your vacation.

WHEN TO PLANT Plant the weigelas, spireas, catmints, phlox, stonecrops, and sweet alyssum after the average date of your last spring frost and when soil has drained sufficiently to be dug.

PEAK DISPLAY Springtime, when the weigelas and spireas juxtapose pink and red flowers with wine-purple foliage; late in the season these are joined by the blue flowers of the catmints. A second peak comes in fall, when the sweet alyssum and annual phloxes are mingling their perfumed blossoms with the chartreuse leaves of the Mexican stonecrops and the crisp green, textured foliage of the catmints.

Gardener's Hint

If the annuals—phlox, stonecrops, sweet alyssum—are looking shabby by late summer, shear them back to promote a burst of fresh, new growth.

INGREDIENTS

A **2 WEIGELAS;** *Weigela florida* SPILLED WINE® (mature height and spread 24–36 in.)

B **4 SPIREAS;** *Spiraea japonica* DOUBLE PLAY® Red (mature height and spread 24–36 in.)

C **4 CATMINTS;** *Nepeta faassenii* 'Cat's Meow' (mature height 17–20 in., spread 12–18 in.)

SUBSTITUTIONS

To adjust this garden for a partially shaded spot, replace the weigelas with Kodiak Black diervilla, and the catmints with Magic Show 'Hocus Pocus' or 'Enchanted Indigo' spike speedwells.

Veronica MAGIC SHOW® 'Hocus Pocus'

Diervilla rivularis KODIAK® Black

Veronica MAGIC SHOW® 'Enchanted Indigo'

DIRECTIONS

1. First arrange and plant the shrubs (the weigelas and spireas) to serve as a frame and background for the perennial and annual flowers. Allow each weigela a space 3–4 feet across, and the spireas a space of 2–4 feet.

2. Next mass the catmints and phloxes along the front of the shrubs. The catmints require a spacing of 12–18 inches each, and the phloxes need 10–12 inches each.

3. Create a mixed edging around the garden with the Mexican stonecrops and sweet alyssum. Allow the stonecrops a spacing of 8–12 inches each, and the sweet alyssum 12–18 inches each.

D **7 PHLOXES;** *Phlox drumondii* INTENSIA® Red Hot (mature height and spread 10–16 in.)

E **9 MEXICAN STONECROPS;** *Sedum mexicanum* LEMON CORAL™ (mature height 3–10 in., spread 10–14 in.)

F **9 SWEET ALYSSUM;** *Lobularia* WHITE KNIGHT® (mature height 4–6 in., spread 18–24 in.)

PLANTING GUIDE

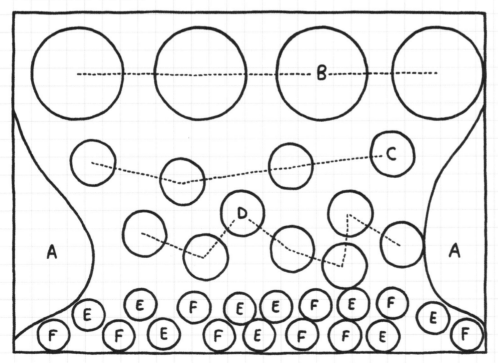

Deer-Resistant Garden

TOTAL SPACE REQUIRED **120 square feet** • SITE **Full sun** • HARDINESS **Zones 4–8**

NOTHING IS MORE discouraging than planting a beautiful garden only for voracious deer to graze it to nubbins. Fortunately, you can take steps to discourage these destructive visitors. Surrounding your garden with deer-proof fencing is an option, albeit an expensive one. Less costly and usually effective in discouraging deer visits is stocking your garden with plants that deer do not typically favor as food.

This is not a guarantee; if deer become hungry enough they will eat practically anything. But under ordinary circumstances, deer will turn up their noses at the plants recommended here. Follow this recipe and you will enjoy a wealth of flowers and colorful foliage, without (in most cases) significant deer damage.

WHEN TO PLANT Plant the coral bells after the average date of your last spring frost and when soil has drained sufficiently to be dug. Plant the annuals (summer snapdragons, lantanas, euphorbias, and petunias) when daytime and nighttime temperatures remain at or above 60°F.

PEAK DISPLAY This combination offers abundant color and interest from spring through fall, with winter color provided by the evergreen coral bells.

Gardener's Hint

Deer are creatures of habit who follow the same trails for generations. Locate where they are entering your property, and block the entryway with large deer-resistant shrubs, such as Cardinal Candy viburnum, which grows to 6–8 feet tall.

INGREDIENTS

A **8 SUMMER SNAPDRAGONS;** *Angelonia* ANGELFACE® Perfectly Pink (mature height 18–30 in., spread 12–18 in.)

B **3 CORAL BELLS;** *Heuchera* PRIMO® 'Black Pearl' (mature height 18–20 in., spread 26–30 in.)

SUBSTITUTIONS

Deer's food preferences vary somewhat from region to region. If any of the recommended plants should prove vulnerable in your area, try substituting other deer-resistant Proven Winners plants such as Pearl Glam beautyberry, Lil' Miss Sunshine blue-beard, or Decadence Lemon Meringue false indigo.

Caryopteris ×clandonensis LIL' MISS SUNSHINE®

Baptisia DECADENCE® 'Lemon Meringue'

Callicarpa PEARL GLAM®

DIRECTIONS

1. Place and plant the summer snapdragons, allowing each plant a space 10–14 inches across.

2. Set out the black-leaved coral bells to create a series of eye-catching focal points, allowing each coral bells a space 26–30 inches across.

3. Fill in with annuals, allowing 20–30 inches for each lantana, 10–12 inches for each euphorbia, and 8–12 inches for each petunia.

C **5 LANTANAS;** *Lantana camara* LUSCIOUS® BERRY BLEND™ (mature height 18–30 in., spread 20–30 in.)

D **6 EUPHORBIAS;** *Euphorbia* DIAMOND FROST® (mature height and spread 12–18 in.)

E **8 PETUNIAS;** *Petunia* SUPERTUNIA® Sangria Charm (mature height 6–12 in., spread 12–18 in.)

PLANTING GUIDE

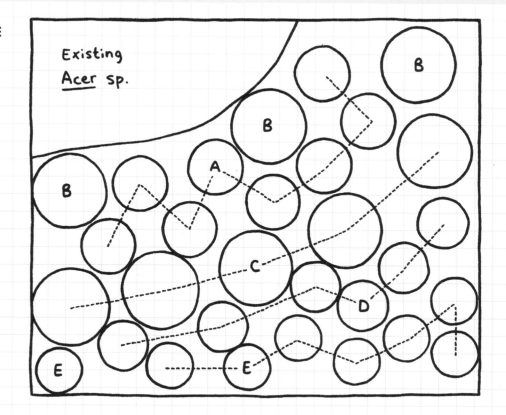

Existing
Acer sp.

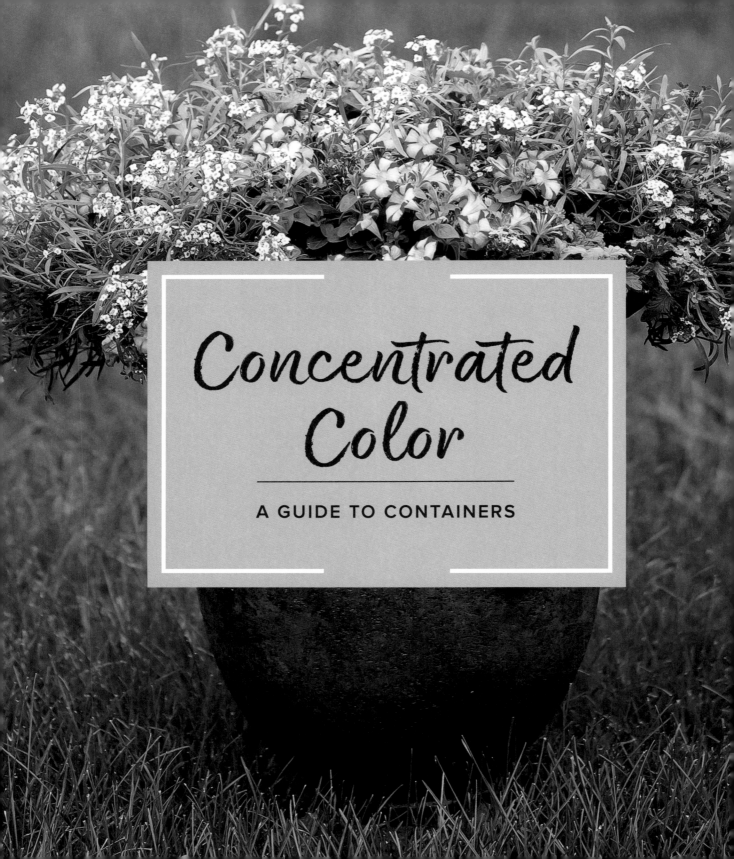

Concentrated Color

A GUIDE TO CONTAINERS

GETTING STARTED WITH CONTAINERS

Containers are the spice that brings landscapes to life. And like a spice, you don't need many colorful containers to energize a whole yard. Just a pair of flower-filled tubs flanking the front steps, for example, turns a mere doorway into an elegant entrance. Hang a basket of blooms over the porch railing or from the tree that shades the deck, and you'll find yourself eye-to-eye with beauty every time you step outside. Set an urn-full of annuals in the middle of the backyard and what was just space instantly becomes a view.

On the fence about whether to add containers to your outdoor space? Here are some of the top reasons to include:

- **VERSATILITY:** Container gardening allows you to have flowers and foliage wherever it will please the eye—on the pavement, in the air, anywhere a spot of color is needed.

- **BIG IMPACT FOR LOW COST:** Nestling plants in a container is like putting a statue on a pedestal. By raising the plants above their surroundings, you increase their visual importance, so that a half dozen flowers blooming together in a tub is likely to have the same impact as a bed-full in the ground.

- **EASY CARE:** Container plantings involve no backbreaking deep digging of beds and barely any weeding. Regular watering (along with the periodic dose of fertilizer) is a must, but otherwise maintenance is reduced to an occasional pinching off of faded flowers.

◄ A ceramic footed urn, outfitted with petunias, verbenas, and sweet alyssum, beckons with fragrance and lush beauty.

- **IDEAL FOR EXPERIMENTATION:** Containers are portable; if you don't like the effect of that basket in one spot, hang it in another. Assemble your smaller baskets and pots around the patio for the night of the birthday or other party—then redistribute them in the garden the next day.

- **SAFETY FROM PESTS:** If your garden is plagued by gophers, rabbits, or deer, elevating the flowers in hanging baskets or cultivating them on the safety of an enclosed deck is the easiest way to protect them against hungry visitors.

▶ A stylish black-and-white combination dresses up the doorstep.

DESIGNING WITH CONTAINERS

No other kind of gardening offers the same design opportunities as container cultivation. In general, your containers should reflect not only your own sense of style, but also that of the house or building around which they are placed. By matching your containers to the style and colors of the setting, you'll achieve an air of coordinated charm. An Italian terra cotta pot, for example, harmonizes beautifully with a brick wall or terrace. But if the container style clashes with the house style, each will detract from the other. Modern angular stainless steel pots, for example, would probably look out of place in front of a rustic cottage in the country. Likewise, wooden whiskey barrels would do little to enhance a contemporary steel-and-glass house.

A GUIDE TO CONTAINERS AND STYLE

MATERIAL	WEIGHT	NOTES ON USE	COMPATIBLE ARCHITECTURAL STYLES
Fiberglass and resin	Lightweight	Resilient but liable to damage from sharp impacts	Molded in a huge selection of styles with a variety of surface textures. Sometimes used to simulate more expensive materials such as stone or terra cotta.
Metal (steel, aluminum, brass, lead, etc.)	Lightweight (except for lead)	Strong and durable, but may be subject to rust, scratching, or tarnishing	Available in bold modern styles ideal for contemporary-style houses; more traditional styles often suited to period houses—Victorian, Federal, or brick colonials.
Plastic	Lightweight	Resilient, frost- and damp-proof, but prone to deteriorate with prolonged exposure to sunlight	Virtually unlimited selection of forms, colors, and surface textures; can harmonize with any style of architecture. Practical and inexpensive but seldom convincing when used to simulate more expensive traditional materials.

(continued)

MATERIAL	WEIGHT	NOTES ON USE	COMPATIBLE ARCHITECTURAL STYLES
Wood	Lightweight to moderate	Vulnerable to damp and decay; best used with double potting	Wooden containers are easily made to order so can harmonize with many styles; especially good for colonial or ranch houses.
Terra cotta	Heavy	Relatively fragile, liable to damage by freezing if not treated with a waterproofing product	Mediterranean—Italianate, French, Spanish; unadorned terra cotta pots are at home in rustic cottage settings.
Ceramic (including stoneware)	Moderately heavy	Less fragile than terra cotta, but best protected from frost	Ideally suited to stone or brick houses, but depending on glaze and form, ceramic containers can harmonize with bold, modern architecture, Asian-style houses, rustic country cottages, and even Victorian or Craftsman homes.
Concrete	Very heavy	Brittle, chips easily, not easily moved	A versatile material that can be tinted and cast with a variety of aggregates (pebbles, crushed stone, coarse sand, etc.) for widely different looks. Often used as an inexpensive substitute for stone.
Stone	Very heavy	Massive and brittle, not easily moved	More roughly finished examples are suited to contemporary or Japanese-style settings or woodland gardens; more polished, ornate specimens are at home in formal settings.

These containers are commonly made out of plastic but may also be wire baskets lined with coconut fiber, which is also known as coir. Coco-lined baskets offer superior drainage and air permeability, but also tend to dry out more quickly than plastic hanging baskets. When using coco-lined baskets be sure to soak the liners for at least 30 seconds before filling these containers with potting mix—otherwise the liner will steal moisture from the potting mix and the roots of any newly potted plants.

▲ Plants whose roots require very well-drained soil—like these succulents—will adapt better to life in a porous container, where moisture can move out directly through the walls, than in a plastic or fiberglass container, which tends to trap moisture in the soil.

COORDINATING CONTAINER AND PLANTING

Your choice of containers should coordinate with the needs of the plants, since no planting looks good when it's not thriving. Porous containers, notably those made of terra cotta or other unglazed ceramics or unsealed concrete, allow water to move outward from the soil through the walls of the pot. Drought-tolerant plants such as rosemary, lavender, and most other culinary herbs, as well as succulents, especially appreciate such containers. The downside of porous pots is that they allow plantings to dry out more rapidly than those in non-porous pots; however, they are more forgiving if over-watered. Plastic, fiberglass, metal, and ceramic containers are non-porous. Plantings in such pots dry out more slowly but are liable to become waterlogged when over-watered. This is likely to injure or even kill the affected plants.

CONTAINER PLANTING DESIGN TIPS

When designing a container planting, select plants that have compatible needs (light conditions, moisture requirements, hardiness), so that they will grow well together. The combination of colors and textures you select is a matter of taste, but a few points are particularly useful to keep in mind.

- The smaller the container, the simpler your design should be. A compact pot filled with a single type of flower or foliage plant generally looks better than a pot jammed with, say, one red flower, one white flower, and one blue flower.

- If you do choose to combine two or more different types of flowers in a small container, choose ones with related colors—different shades of pink, for example, or blues.

- With a larger container where a more varied planting is practical, include plants of different heights and patterns of growth by following the "thriller, filler, spiller" model. That is, place a tall and dramatic plant (the thriller) at the center of the container, surround it with mounding, medium-tall plants (the fillers), and plant low-growing, spreading plants (the spillers) around the perimeter to spill over the container's edge.

- Pay attention to foliages. Many plants such as coleus and New Guinea impatiens owe their color more to leaves than flowers. Foliage can also be a source of appealing textures—you can't look at the soft, silvery foliage of dusty miller (*Senecio cineraria*) without wanting to stroke it.

CONTAINERS AND DRAINAGE

Plants require that their roots be allowed to breathe, which means that they do not thrive in waterlogged soil. The simplest way to prevent this is to make sure that the container has drainage holes in the bottom, so that excess water can run off.

If you have a beautiful container with no drainage holes, you can try the double-pot solution. Select a pot with drainage holes that is small enough to fit inside the decorative but drainage-less container. Plant into the smaller pot, then set it inside the larger container, resting it on a layer of gravel. You can fill the remaining space between the two pots, if large, with perlite to stabilize the inner pot and eliminate wobbling.

(Double-potting can also be used to protect attractive but perishable containers. When working with wooden containers, double-potting is a smart step. Or,

◄ Thriller Let's Dance Blue Jangles hydrangea takes center stage in this blue on blue recipe, with flossflowers, fan flowers, and dwarf morning glories filling in and spilling out of the container.

take a wickerwork plant stand, for example. This wouldn't last long in direct contact with the soil, but by lining it with a waterproof plastic container, it becomes a practical and durable home for a plant arrangement.)

Another option for containers without drainage holes is to create a reservoir. Put a layer of pebbles, pot shards, gravel, or even foam peanuts at the bottom of the drainage-less container. This layer acts as a reservoir to absorb excess water, letting it drain out of the soil. The depth of reservoir needed depends on the depth of the pot, but do not skimp. Before adding soil, cover the reservoir with a layer of porous material such as fiberglass screening or landscape fabric.

If you choose not to use either of these options, you may decide to go ahead and just drill a hole in the base of your container. Be aware that ceramic, plastic, or resin vessels are subject to splitting, thus ruining the item. Clay containers are prone to cracking but can be drilled using the correct bit for the drill and working very carefully.

PREPARING THE CONTAINER

The plants are bought, the container selected, and you are ready to go. Before you start planting, however, you must attend to a few preliminaries.

In most cases, new, fresh-from-the-store containers are fine to use as is. But you should soak terra cotta or porous ceramic containers in water for several hours before use to leach out any chemicals left over from the manufacturing process, and to saturate the absorbent walls of the pots. Otherwise, when filled with plants, the containers will immediately draw water from the soil, denying water to the roots of the newly installed plants.

When reusing a container, it's important to clean it thoroughly before planting. Containers made of non-absorbent materials such as metals, plastics, and fiberglass just need to be scrubbed with soapy water and rinsed with clean water. Containers made of absorbent materials, such as terra cotta or porous ceramic, are likely to be encrusted with mineral salts—look for the white stains on the walls of the pots. To remove, soak the pots in a solution of 10 parts water to 1 part chlorine bleach (wear rubber gloves and follow all safety cautions on the bleach container). Scrub, if necessary, with a nylon scrubber or nail brush, rinse thoroughly with clean water, and air dry.

SELECTING A POTTING MIX

The most important step to success when growing any plant is to provide it with suitable soil. This is especially critical for container plantings, whose roots cannot reach beyond the small quantity of soil contained in the pot, basket, or tub.

Ordinary garden soil is not suitable for container-grown plants. The frequent soakings and the extra-heavy demands that container plantings make on soil fertility soon reduce even the best loam to compacted mud. Most packaged soil-based potting mixes are little better. Their contents vary with the whims of the packager, so their fertility is unpredictable. Like garden soils, soil-based potting mixes are liable to become compacted and waterlogged.

Container plantings fare far better when potted into a packaged *soilless* mix. These are composed of carefully assembled combinations of some organic base, such as sphagnum peat, with other organic elements including bark, and inorganic elements like perlite (an expanded volcanic rock) or vermiculite (expanded mica), which ensure good drainage while protecting against compaction. A properly formulated soilless potting mix absorbs water readily, but also drains quickly. Thus, plants grown in it are, if watered properly, assured of enough but not too much moisture.

Soilless mixes are also sterile—free from weed seeds, and plant pests and diseases. Unlike true soils, they have no nutrient value, though many are mixed with fertilizer before they are packaged. Plants grown in soilless mixes, therefore, require regular feeding if they are to thrive.

Soilless potting mixes should be moistened before use. When very dry, as they usually are in the package, cold water is not absorbed readily. Instead, add hot water (as hot as it comes from the tap) and stir it in with a trowel until the mix is as moist as a wrung-out sponge.

WATER-CONSERVING ADDITIVES

Gardeners often find it difficult to keep up with the frequent watering requirements of container plantings. If you find this to be the case, try experimenting with two products that help retain water and reduce the need for irrigation when mixed into the soilless potting mix.

- **POLYMER GELS:** Marketed under a variety of brand names, these crystals absorb and hold a large volume of water which

▲ Labeling can vary, so be sure to check that your potting mix is designed for containers. This Proven Winners potting "soil" is actually peat and bark based, a great option for a soilless mix.

Self-Watering Containers

If you are unable or unwilling to check on your container plantings daily, "self-watering" containers may be a good choice. Such containers are equipped with reservoirs in their base, which you replenish with water periodically through easy-fill holes. Water wicks upward through the soil to the plant roots. You can add diluted fertilizer to the water in the reservoir to make the container self-feeding as well.

they release gradually to the plants. Mix the dry gel into the soilless potting mix before planting, at a rate of ½ teaspoon per quart of mix. Fill the bottom third of the container with this gel/potting mix blend, then top up with pure potting mix. Water the container twice within a period of a couple of hours to hydrate the gel before planting.

- **COCONUT FIBER OR COIR:** An agricultural by-product, this natural, organic material is ordinarily sold compressed into blocks. When soaked for an hour in a bucket of water, a block softens into a spongy mass. If you break up the block and blend the fiber into the soilless potting mix prior to planting, it increases the ability of the mix to absorb and retain water by as much as one third. Use with caution: acid-loving plants such as azaleas react well to coir, but some others, notably impatiens and coleus, do not.

POTTING UP, STEP BY STEP

Before you begin, take note: If you plan to move tubs or large containers around, place them on a wheeled plant caddy or dolly *before* you fill them with soil and plants.

1. Cover the bottom of the container with a piece of fiberglass window screening or the porous landscape fabric commonly sold at garden centers to suppress weed growth (for small pots, use a coffee filter). This barrier will prevent the potting mix from leaking out through the container's drainage holes, and will also stop small pests from entering through the bottom.

2. In a pan, bucket, or other suitable container, moisten the soilless potting mix with hot water until it is as damp as a wrung-out sponge. If the potting mix is not pretreated with a fertilizer, blend in a slow-release fertilizer formulated for container-grown plants. If using polymer gels or other water-conserving additives, blend them with the potting mix at this time, and then dampen it all.

3. Fill the container to within 3–4 inches of its top with the moistened, amended potting mix.

4. Slip the plants gently out of their nursery containers. If you find the roots coiled around the bottom of the root ball, take a sharp knife and slit the roots vertically in four places at equal intervals around the root ball.

5. Arrange the plants according to your design within the container. To accommodate larger plants, you may need to scoop out shallow holes in the potting

mix. Make sure that the tops of all the root balls reach the same level, about 1 inch below the top of the container.

6. Fill in around the root balls with more moistened potting mix. Press in the mix gently with your fingertips to eliminate any air pockets. The potting mix should be firmly packed but not compressed.

7. Water the planted containers thoroughly, until water runs out of the drainage holes in the bottom. You may have to repeat this process to ensure even wetting.

8. Before moving a container to its intended location, keep it for a few days in a bright, sheltered spot out of direct sunlight to allow plants to recover from the shock of planting.

MAINTENANCE OF CONTAINER PLANTS

The most important task in maintaining any container planting is irrigation. Because their root systems are confined, an established container planting can be amazingly efficient at removing moisture from its potting mix, and in summertime you may well find yourself watering daily or even twice a day. The larger and more impressive the growth becomes, of course, the more frequent the need for irrigation. However, be careful not to over-water; keeping the potting mix perpetually soaked will stunt root growth and is likely to cause the plants to rot and die eventually.

Fertilization also takes on a special importance with container plantings. If you mixed some slow-release fertilizer into the potting mix when you installed the plants, then the plants should be set for a period of weeks. If you failed to fertilize at that time or used a quick-release product, then the plants in the container will need feeding much sooner. In either case, you will notice a slowing in the growth of the plants and, typically, a diminution of flowering. That signals a renewed need for fertilization.

When you fertilize, we recommend that you do so in a way that releases the nutrients at a slow and gradual rate. One way to accomplish this is to use a soluble, quick-release fertilizer at half the recommended rate, but apply it twice as often as recommended. A simpler and superior way to achieve the same end is to use a slow-release product that releases nutrients at a rate and

Drainage Dos and Don'ts

Do: To ensure free drainage, place containers on "pot feet" or bricks to raise them off the surface of the deck or patio. Place small containers on up-turned pots.

Don't: The traditional practice of filling the bottom of the container with pebbles or pieces of broken pots "to promote drainage" has been proven by recent research to actually impede the escape of excess water through the drainage holes.

balance ideally tailored for container plant growth. It should be marked on the product label.

Whatever fertilizer you use, avoid giving a container planting more than it needs—it is best to observe the feeding schedule recommended on the product package. If you hope to overwinter your plants in regions with cold winters, it is wise to stop fertilizing at midsummer, to discourage your plants from producing frost-vulnerable new growth in fall.

CONTROLLING GROWTH

Vigorous growth of the plants in your containers is your aim, of course, but it brings with it another maintenance concern. If you start with premium stock and give it good care, a container planting may soon outgrow its space. Or the plants may just extend their branches until they are straggling or unsightly. In either case, you'll need to take steps to address the situation.

The most likely offenders in this situation are the fastest-growing plants. That means perennials and, especially, annuals. Shrubs are slower growing and if you selected one carefully to match the size of the container, you ought to be able to leave it in place for at least a year before you need to replace it—at which time you can recycle the shrub by transplanting it into the landscape.

If the trouble-maker is an annual or even a perennial, you can usually correct the situation by clipping back the overly long branches with a sharp pair of shears. Such a "haircut" forces the plants to push out new growth, thus refreshing the appearance of the planting as a whole; typically, it also leads to a vigorous resurgence of flowering. Indeed, if you shear back a perennial right after it has bloomed, you may encourage the plant to produce a second, albeit smaller, flush of flowers.

OVERWINTERING CONTAINERS IN COLD CLIMATES

True annuals such as zinnias or sweet alyssum are genetically programmed to survive just one year: after they reach maturity and bloom, they set seed and die. Trying to overwinter such plants to use them again in the spring is guaranteed to fail. Some other popular plants suitable for containers are actually tropical or sub-tropical perennials that cannot stand the winter cold in most of North America, and so are grown for just a single season as annuals. This group—which includes petunias, calibrachoas, impatiens, and coleuses—can be overwintered indoors, ideally in a greenhouse or heated sunroom, but rarely with results good enough to justify the extra work. However, they can brighten a heated sunroom or conservatory during the colder months.

Hardy shrubs and hardy perennials, plants such as hydrangeas and coral bells that naturally overwinter outdoors in climates like those of North America, are the most practical plants for overwintering in containers. If you have selected types hardy in your USDA zone, these plants should be able to handle the cold that most winters will throw at them. Here are some steps to take in order to protect them from winter winds, rapid temperature swings, and thaws followed by quick freezes, which are stressful for dormant plants.

1. Cut back spent perennials, and mulch them with straw to protect plants against extreme weather. Remember to remove the mulch just as the buds swell in spring.

2. Where winters are very cold (zone 6 and north) wrap each container in bubble wrap or several layers of burlap to protect it from splitting due to frost. Group all of your containers together next to the foundation of your house or in another sheltered location. Once the pots are gathered, surround them with bales of straw, fill the resulting enclosure with loose straw, and cover the whole with a secured plastic tarp.

3. If a plant is of questionable hardiness in your climate, move the container to a protected indoor spot such as a shed or an unheated garage, next to an inside wall. This is also the best practice for any plants in ceramic containers, which are most likely to shatter when they freeze, or split from the pressure of the potting mix, which expands as it freezes.

4. Check the planted containers periodically. When the potting mix becomes very dry, water just enough to keep it barely damp. Do not move the containers back outdoors until the danger of frost is past in spring.

Rather than going to all this trouble, you may decide to simply empty your containers in the fall; store them in the basement, garage, or shed over the winter, and replant them in spring. If you opt to do this, you can transplant all the hardy perennials and shrubs from your containers to a garden bed in early fall. By late fall the plants will have gone dormant. Cover them then with a blanket of straw or evergreen boughs to help them weather their first winter outdoors, and to keep the frost from heaving the new plants up and out of the soil, exposing the roots to drying out. Coral bells are especially prone to heaving.

Twenty-Five Container Recipes

◄ Supertunia Trailing Strawberry Pink Veined makes a delicate and graceful spiller for this container.

Trick-or-Treat

CONTAINER TYPE **Black metal cauldron**
CONTAINER SIZE **15 inches across × 11 inches deep** • SITE **Full sun to part shade**

HAPPY HALLOWEEN! Even if you are not hosting a spooky party you will want to dress up your garden for the seasonal festivities. This recipe—planted in a black witch's cauldron—is perfect for any partially shaded spots.

Foliage colors and textures are important elements in the design of any container. Here, they are the backbone of the display, which features several fast-growing annuals: dark-leaved Graceful Grasses Vertigo purple fountain grass, ColorBlaze Sedona Sunset coleus with jack-o-lantern orange leaves, and Sweet Caroline Bewitched After Midnight sweet potato vine spilling swags of artfully cut foliage, inky as a black cat. The orange and yellow flowers of Campfire Fireburst bidens enliven what might otherwise be a somber picture. These plants all tolerate part shade, but the sweet potato vine and fountain grass, like most black-leaved plants, exhibit the best, darkest color in bright light—in lower light their foliage will be tinged with green.

Gardener's Hint

Pinch off the growing tips of the coleus and sweet potato vine at planting time to encourage denser, more luxuriant growth.

INGREDIENTS

A **1 PURPLE FOUNTAIN GRASS;** *Pennisetum purpureum* GRACEFUL GRASSES® VERTIGO®

B **1 COLEUS;** *Solenostemon scutellarioides* COLORBLAZE® SEDONA SUNSET™

C **3 SWEET POTATO VINES;** *Ipomoea batatas* Sweet Caroline Bewitched AFTER MIDNIGHT™

D **2 BIDENS;** *Bidens* CAMPFIRE® Fireburst

PLANTING GUIDE

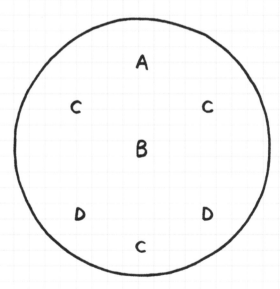

SUBSTITUTIONS

Where cold weather comes early in the fall, substitute an Orange Symphony African daisy for the frost-sensitive coleus, and Primo 'Black Pearl' coral bells plants for the sweet potato vines. With these substitutions the design depends more upon flowers than foliage but is still dramatic.

Osteospermum Orange Symphony

Heuchera PRIMO® 'Black Pearl'

Welcome to Spring

CONTAINER TYPE Coco-lined hanging basket
CONTAINER SIZE 12 inches across × 10 inches deep • **SITE** Full sun

SPRING BRINGS a hunger for flowers, but plants need to be able to tolerate a wide range of temperatures in order to flourish in this fickle season of frosty nights and mornings mixed with sunny, warm days. This recipe focuses on the best of the recent flower breeding programs: plants that mature and bloom quickly even in chilly weather, yet hang on through warm weather to prolong their display into early summer.

Pansies, for example, are a traditional springtime flower, but they quickly fade when the weather heats up. In this recipe we've substituted "pansiolas," updated relatives of pansies with more delicate flowers but a stronger constitution so that they tolerate a light frost as well as early summer warmth. Lobelias and nemesias are also traditional springtime favorites, historically tolerant of cold but not heat. However, like the pansiolas, the selections recommended here have been bred to succeed in both types of weather, to give this basket a longer season of beauty.

Gardener's Hint

If your spring flowers begin to straggle as the weather warms, don't be afraid to shear them back—this will prompt a burst of fresher and more compact new growth.

INGREDIENTS

A **2 PANSIOLAS;** *Viola ×wittrockiana* ANYTIME® Iris

B **2 NEMESIAS;** *Nemesia* SUNSATIA® Lemon

C **2 LOBELIAS;** *Lobelia erinus* LAGUNA® Sky Blue

PLANTING GUIDE

```
      C       B
         A
   B       A    C
```

SUBSTITUTIONS

If any of these early birds fail as the weather heats up, don't hesitate to swap them out for hardier summer annuals. Favorites include Superbells Yellow and Superbells Grape Punch calibrachoas, or Blue My Mind dwarf morning glories.

Calibrachoa SUPERBELLS® Yellow

Calibrachoa SUPERBELLS® GRAPE PUNCH™

Evolvulus BLUE MY MIND®

Basket of Easter or Passover Bloom

CONTAINER TYPE **Oval wooden basket**
CONTAINER SIZE **18 inches long** × **12 inches wide** × **6 inches deep** • SITE **Full sun**

AN ARRANGEMENT DESIGNED to delight the nose as well as the eye, this basket of early flowers is the perfect way to celebrate any spring event. Keep it for yourself or charm your host with it as a house gift. It thrives in any sunny spot.

This container is anchored by a Bloomerang Purple lilac, an innovative dwarf shrub that, like traditional lilacs, blooms generously—and fragrantly—for a couple of weeks in the spring. But then, unlike old-fashioned lilacs, it also reblooms repeatedly from midsummer until frost. Backing up the lilac are two annuals that can shrug off a light frost and which flower steadily throughout the spring: Opal Innocence nemesia engulfs with its cloud of pink-tinged, pale lavender, snapdragon-like blooms, and makes the perfect foil for the royal purple of Laguna Ultraviolet lobelia. These spring bloomers will fade as summer settles in—to prolong this container's display, replace the nemesia and lobelia with heat-tolerant summer annuals. When fall's chilly weather puts an end to this container's show, transplant the lilac to a sunny spot in the garden so that you can enjoy its fragrant blooms for years to come.

Gardener's Hint

Deadheading, snipping off fading flower heads, will prolong and increase the lilac's bloom.

INGREDIENTS

A **1 LILAC;** *Syringa* BLOOMERANG® Purple

B **4 NEMESIAS;** *Nemesia fruticans* Opal INNOCENCE®

C **4 LOBELIAS;** *Lobelia erinus* LAGUNA® ULTRAVIOLET™

PLANTING GUIDE

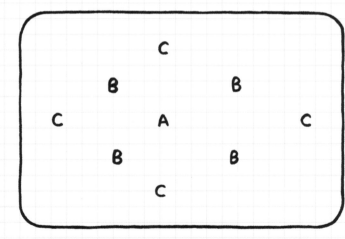

SUBSTITUTIONS

When the nemesias and lobelias fade as the summer heat settles in, replace them with more heat-tolerant summer-blooming annuals such as Supertunia Picasso in Purple petunia and Intensia Blueberry phlox. The phlox is fragrant and will make an outstanding counterpoint to the lilac's second blooming.

Petunia SUPERTUNIA® PICASSO IN PURPLE®

Phlox INTENSIA® Blueberry

Winter Annuals for the South

CONTAINER TYPE Coco-lined hanging basket
CONTAINER SIZE 12 inches across × 10 inches deep • **SITE** Full sun

WINTER IS DEFINITELY a season for flowers in southern gardens—just plant this basket and see. In southern climates (USDA zones 8–11) winter rarely dips to truly cold, with only occasional, modest frosts. The weather of a Deep South winter, in fact, is remarkably similar to northern springs. Thus, plants known as spring annuals in the North work well for winter color in the Deep South. For best results, set the planted container in a sunny spot protected from the wind.

The showy yellow blossoms of Superbells Yellow calibrachoa intermingle with the warm orange-and-red snapdragon-like blossoms of Sunsatia Blood Orange nemesia. With flowers as intensely hued as the name suggests, Laguna Ultraviolet lobelia provides drama and contrast surrounding the other flowers and spilling over the basket edges.

Gardener's Hint

Plant growth is less robust in cool conditions, so take care not to over-water (cold, soaking soil is a sure prescription for root rot) and fertilize sparingly.

INGREDIENTS

A **2 CALIBRACHOAS;**
Calibrachoa SUPERBELLS®
Yellow

B **2 NEMESIAS;** *Nemesia* SUNSATIA®
BLOOD ORANGE™

C **2 LOBELIAS;** *Lobelia erinus*
LAGUNA® ULTRAVIOLET™

PLANTING GUIDE

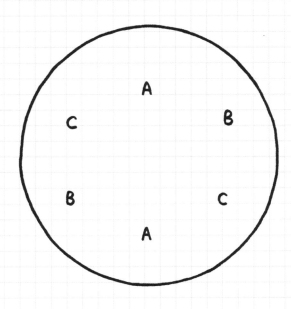

SUBSTITUTIONS

Alternatives for the recommended flowers include Anytime Sunlight or Anytime Iris pansiolas and Dark Knight or 'Blushing Princess' sweet alyssum.

Viola ×*wittrockiana*
ANYTIME® Sunlight

Viola ×*wittrockiana*
ANYTIME® Iris

Lobularia DARK KNIGHT™

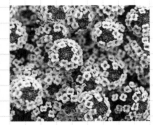

Lobularia BLUSHING
PRINCESS®

Extending the Season into Fall

CONTAINER TYPE **Chipwood farm basket**
CONTAINER SIZE **14 inches across × 6.5 inches deep** • SITE **Full sun**

CHILDREN BACK TO SCHOOL? Ease yourself into autumn with this sun-loving blend of fall colors and contrasting textures. Ripe grasses are the stars of fall, and here the Graceful Grasses 'Rubrum' purple fountain grass strikes just the right note with its purple leaves and tall, arching plumes of delicate seed heads. Easy-to-grow, daisy-like Campfire Fireburst bidens echoes the orange and golden colors of autumn leaves, complemented in this design by clear sun-yellow Superbells calibrachoa. Chameleon-like Supertunia Honey ties the color scheme together with its incredible, ever-changing array of yellow, orange, salmon, and pink blooms. The mounding, well-branched plants thrive in heat and bloom vigorously in summertime, but also continue through cool nights into fall.

Gardener's Hint

The growth of your plants will slow as the weather cools so be careful not to over-water or over-fertilize. A good rule of thumb is to hold off on the fertilizer after Labor Day.

INGREDIENTS

A **1 PURPLE FOUNTAIN GRASS;** *Pennisetum setaceum* GRACEFUL GRASSES® 'Rubrum'

B **2 PETUNIAS;** *Petunia* SUPERTUNIA® HONEY™

C **2 CALIBRACHOAS;** *Calibrachoa* SUPERBELLS® Yellow

D **2 BIDENS;** *Bidens* CAMPFIRE® Fireburst

PLANTING GUIDE

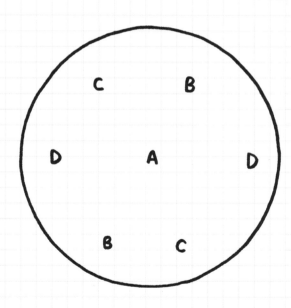

SUBSTITUTIONS

For a display that will thrive in part shade—that is, shade for a few hours daily—replace the purple fountain grass with a Pure White Butterfly marguerite daisy, and replace the bidens with Superbena Royale Peachy Keen.

Argyranthemum frutescens PURE WHITE BUTTERFLY®

Verbena SUPERBENA ROYALE® Peachy Keen

Hummingbird Feeding Station

CONTAINER TYPE **Tapering black metal tub**
CONTAINER SIZE **12 inches across × 5.5 inches deep** • SITE **Full sun**

WATCHING HUMMINGBIRDS sip nectar is enchanting to children and adults alike, but unless you clean your hummingbird feeder and replace the sugar-water regularly, you endanger the health of your feathered visitors. That's why it's much better to feed your hummingbirds the natural way—with a basketful of flowers.

Red and orange, the colors most attractive to these creatures, are also the colors of the tubular blossoms that Vermillionaire large firecracker plant bears from spring to the first fall frost, which makes this annual a hummingbird magnet. Adding a yellow note, the tiny, trumpet-shaped, banana yellow blossoms of Luscious Bananarama lantana are perfectly designed for long hummingbird beaks. The self-cleaning flowers of Supertunia Really Red are also sure to catch the eye of any passing hummer. You'll appreciate the heat and drought tolerance of these plants that keep blooming right through summer's hottest days.

Gardener's Hint

Be sure to provide a shallow birdbath nearby your container—hummingbirds love to bathe and will flit through the spray from fountains and garden misters before perching to preen and fluff.

INGREDIENTS

A **1 LARGE FIRECRACKER PLANT;**
Cuphea VERMILLIONAIRE®

B **2 LANTANAS;** *Lantana camara*
LUSCIOUS® BANANARAMA™

C **2 PETUNIAS;** *Petunia*
SUPERTUNIA® Really Red

PLANTING GUIDE

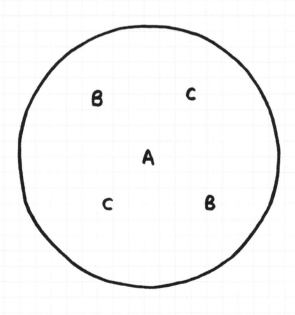

SUBSTITUTIONS

If you cannot obtain a large firecracker plant, substitute an orange-flowered lantana such as Luscious Citrus Blend. Other hummingbird-attracting annuals include Superbells Pomegranate Punch calibrachoa and Artist Purple flossflower.

Lantana camara
LUSCIOUS® CITRUS BLEND™

Calibrachoa SUPERBELLS®
POMEGRANATE PUNCH™

Ageratum ARTIST® Purple

Midsummer Color

CONTAINER TYPE **Modern, oval-shaped resin container**
CONTAINER SIZE **24 inches long × 16 inches wide × 24 inches deep** • SITE **Full sun**

MUCH AS WE LOVE subtle pastels, we know that they show up best in the soft light of spring. To stand up to the brilliant sunshine of July and August, you need strong, bold colors. You need tough plants, too, that can tolerate high temperatures, and drought alternating with humidity. This recipe offers all of this and more. While the rest of your garden may sulk during the dog days, this colorful floral cocktail will shine.

The focal point for this container is Mystic Illusion dahlia—its large, incandescent yellow blossoms are set against dark, almost black, foliage for maximum visual impact. The dahlia may stretch and get leggy. Surround it with mounding Supertunia Royal Velvet petunia plants, which bear their rich purple flowers (magnets for hummingbirds and butterflies) continuously from late spring through early fall. 'Sweet Caroline Light Green' sweet potato vine is the chartreuse waterfall spilling over the container's edge.

Gardener's Hint

Though intolerant of cold, dahlias are perennials that you can save and reuse from year to year. When the first fall frost kills back the foliage, dig out the dahlia tubers (they look like long potatoes). Wash off any soil and allow to air dry. Then wrap the tubers in newspapers and store in a dark, cool (35–45°F), but frost-free place. Replant the following spring after the average date of your last spring frost for another summer of flowers.

INGREDIENTS

A **1 DAHLIA;** *Dahlia* Mystic Illusion

B **4 PETUNIAS;** *Petunia* SUPERTUNIA® ROYAL VELVET®

C **4 SWEET POTATO VINES;** *Ipomoea batatas* 'Sweet Caroline Light Green'

PLANTING GUIDE

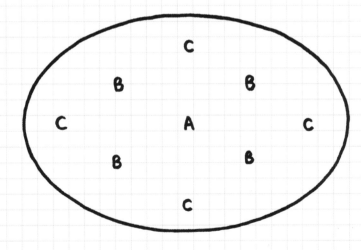

SUBSTITUTIONS

If you want to use this recipe in a semi-shaded spot, replace the dahlia with 'Bottle Rocket' ligularia. You can transplant this perennial, hardy to zones 4–9, to the garden when the container fades in fall.

Ligularia 'Bottle Rocket'

Four-Season Evergreen

CONTAINER TYPE **Terra cotta–style plastic container**
CONTAINER SIZE **24 inches across × 21 inches deep** • SITE **Part shade**

GARDEN ENJOYMENT doesn't have to end with the onset of winter, as this recipe proves. Indeed, this colorful quilt of evergreen foliage is just the pick-me-up for a January morning. You can enjoy this container in a partly shaded spot all year round in zones 4–7. It is advisable to use a plastic container that won't shatter when it freezes.

North Pole arborvitae furnishes a strong, upright focal point around which the recipe revolves. The rich green needles of this durable conifer resist burning from winter winds. The deep purple leaves of Dolce Wildberry coral bells contrast with the burgundy-splashed, chartreuse leaves of Fun and Games Leapfrog foamy bells, together forming a perfect launching pad for the arborvitae.

Gardener's Hint

Winter winds can dehydrate plants when the soil is frozen and moisture in it is unavailable to the roots. Take advantage of winter thaws to water the container thoroughly and deeply.

INGREDIENTS

A **1 ARBORVITAE;** *Thuja occidentalis* NORTH POLE®

B **4 CORAL BELLS;** *Heuchera* DOLCE® Wildberry

C **4 FOAMY BELLS;** *Heucherella* FUN AND GAMES® Leapfrog

PLANTING GUIDE

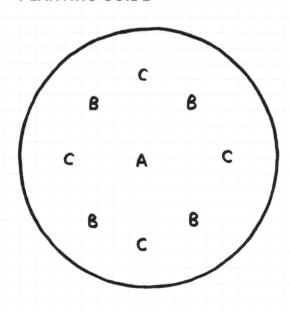

SUBSTITUTIONS

For a container with a more compact, less vertical profile, set Anna's Magic Ball arborvitae in a base of 'Jade Peacock' foamflower and Primo 'Pretty Pistachio' coral bells.

Thuja occidentalis ANNA'S MAGIC BALL®

Tiarella 'Jade Peacock'

Heuchera PRIMO® 'Pretty Pistachio'

Made for the Shade

CONTAINER TYPE **Ceramic bowl**
CONTAINER SIZE **18 inches across × 9 inches deep** • SITE **Part shade to shade**

A SHADY SPOT makes a pleasant retreat in summertime, but it can be visually dim and dull. A dash of white—either foliage or flowers or, as in this case, both—can shine like a beacon to light up the darkness.

Most flowers, although they may survive in part or full shade, do not bloom well in such locations. One solution is to get your color in the shade from bright-hued, tropical foliage. Here, the outsized, green-rimmed leaves of Artful Fire and Ice angel wings sport centers of silvery white, veined with vivid red. The foliage colors are echoed with a pair of exceptional annuals that bloom well even in low light conditions: Endless Flirtation browallias bear blossoms of a luminous white, while Infinity Dark Pink New Guinea impatiens warm what could otherwise be a chilly composition. Heat-lovers all, these plants thrive in conditions of high temperatures and humidity that would daunt lesser plants, making this recipe perfect for the South.

Gardener's Hint

The angel wings and New Guinea impatiens are true tropicals that require warm weather to thrive. If you live in a northern climate, be careful not to plant too early in spring as air temperatures below 50°F will chill and stunt the plants.

INGREDIENTS

A **1 ANGEL WINGS;** *Caladium hortulanum* ARTFUL® FIRE AND ICE™

B **3 BROWALLIAS;** *Browallia* ENDLESS™ Flirtation

C **3 NEW GUINEA IMPATIENS;** *Impatiens hawkeri* INFINITY® Dark Pink

PLANTING GUIDE

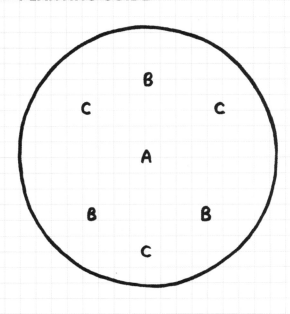

SUBSTITUTIONS

An alternative planting with a similar effect combines Shadowland 'Wheee!' hosta, Primo 'Pistachio' coral bells, and ColorBlaze Dark Star coleus. Both the hosta and coral bells are winter-hardy, to zones 3 and 4, respectively, through zone 9, and may be transplanted to a shady part of the garden in fall as the container reaches the end of its season.

Hosta SHADOWLAND® 'Wheee!'

Heuchera PRIMO® 'Pretty Pistachio'

Solenostemon scutellarioides COLORBLAZE® Dark Star

Fourth of July

CONTAINER TYPE **Ceramic stoneware pot**
CONTAINER SIZE **16 inches across × 18 inches deep** • SITE **Full sun to part shade**

CELEBRATE THE HOLIDAY with a patriotically themed red, white, and blue container. Given minimum care and a sunny or semi-shaded spot, this container will reward with months of festive bloom.

Graceful Grasses 'Skyrocket' fountain grass anchors the display, sending up slender white flowers arching on long stems above a fountain of white-striped leaves. In our enthusiasm for flowers, gardeners tend to forget that foliage is at least as big a factor in the visual impact of a plant, and this is a good example of how foliage can add interest to a container. The red starbursts of the gerbera daisies rise up to present a startling contrast to the grass's pale bloom. Also called Transvaal daisies, in a nod to their South African origin, gerberas are reliable summer bloomers, though they appreciate afternoon shade in hot climates. Supertunia Trailing Blue petunias round out the display. With a naturally trailing habit of growth, this plant is an ideal spiller. If it starts to straggle in late July, cut back the longest stems (no more than one fifth of the total number of stems) to rejuvenate the plant and enhance its bloom.

Gardener's Hint

Adequate irrigation is essential for a good midsummer show—water whenever the potting soil in the container dries out and the plant leaves start to droop. Fertilize at every second or third watering during summer with a water-soluble fertilizer diluted to half the recommended strength to ensure the most abundant bloom.

INGREDIENTS

A **1 FOUNTAIN GRASS;**
Pennisetum setaceum
GRACEFUL GRASSES®
'Sky-rocket'

B **1 GERBERA DAISY;** *Gerbera* red
cultivar

C **3 PETUNIAS;** *Petunia* SUPERTUNIA®
Trailing Blue

PLANTING GUIDE

B   A

C   C

C

SUBSTITUTIONS

For an alternative red, white, and blue arrangement,
surround a Lo & Behold 'Blue Chip' butterfly bush with
Superbena Red and Supertunia White.

Buddleia LO & BEHOLD®
'Blue Chip'

Verbena SUPERBENA® Red

Petunia SUPERTUNIA® White

Hot and Dry

CONTAINER TYPE **Ceramic and stone container**
CONTAINER SIZE **21 inches long × 13 inches wide × 9 inches deep** • SITE **Full sun**

Gardener's Hint

If the lantana shifts gears and begins to produce berries rather than new flowers, shear it back to return it to full bloom.

IF YOUR SUMMERS are scorchers, the combination of heat and drought is liable to curtail the flowering of all but the most summer-proof plants. The flowers in this recipe, however, are as close to heat- and drought-proof as they come, making this an ideal container not only for hot climates but also in cooler ones for that difficult spot next to a sun-drenched south- or west-facing wall. When your other plantings are flagging during the dog days, this one will shine.

Diamond Frost euphorbia may look delicate with its clouds of icy-white flowers, but it's actually tough as nails, a real summer-survivor. It does this with very little care, too: its naturally compact growth means it rarely needs trimming, and it is self-cleaning, shedding its flowers as it ages, so no deadheading is necessary. Luscious Lemonade lantana, another tough plant—and one that attracts butterflies, hummingbirds, and other pollinators—spills gracefully over the lip of the container to add grace to this display. It, too, seldom needs deadheading.

INGREDIENTS

A 2 LANTANAS; *Lantana camara* LUSCIOUS® Lemonade

B 4 EUPHORBIAS; *Euphorbia* DIAMOND FROST®

PLANTING GUIDE

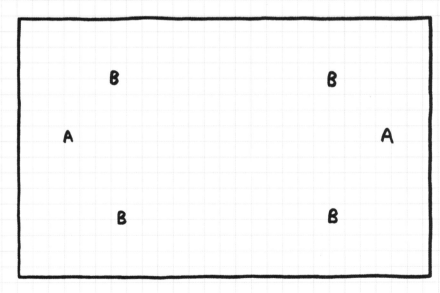

SUBSTITUTIONS

In arid climates, cactus-like succulents may be the best summertime alternatives. In such locales, try planting a succulent container (page 158) for reliable bloom in hot weather seasons.

Doorway Sentinel

CONTAINER TYPE **Square ceramic stoneware planter**
CONTAINER SIZE **24 inches across × 20 inches deep** • SITE **Full sun**

REPETITION is a powerful tool for garden designers; it can be used for emphasis and to create a visual rhythm. This recipe echoes the vertical line of a sunny doorway with a vertically oriented container; the aim is to turn this transition point from house to garden into a target for the eye as well as the feet.

Establish the visual emphasis of the container with a spire-shaped evergreen standing proud and tall like a living exclamation point. Polar Gold arborvitae is just the plant for this: naturally compact and trim, its needles are gilded at the tips to provide a bright and elegant appearance year-round. This arborvitae is also outstandingly winter-proof, reliably hardy as far north as zone 3. To enhance the colors of the evergreen in summertime, yellow-tipped, orange gerbera daisies and pink-edged, golden-flushed trumpets (Supertunia Honey) surround its base. Both of these flowers bloom from late spring through early fall, giving your doorway sentinel long-lasting appeal.

Gardener's Hint

Deadhead the gerbera daisies, snipping off the flowers to the base as they age and start to go to seed, to prolong this plant's display. Transplant the arborvitae (hardy in zones 3–7), to a garden bed when it outgrows the container (it can reach a height of 15 ft.).

INGREDIENTS

A **1 ARBORVITAE;** *Thuja occidentalis* POLAR GOLD®

B **4 GERBERA DAISIES;** *Gerbera* orange cultivar

C **4 PETUNIAS;** *Petunia* SUPERTUNIA® HONEY™

PLANTING GUIDE

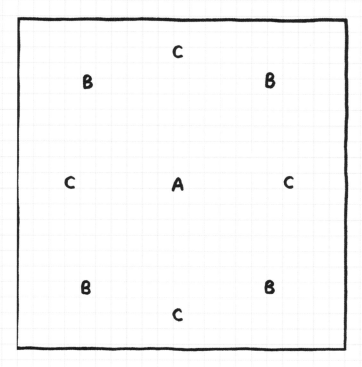

SUBSTITUTIONS

South of zone 7 (in zone 8), replace the less heat-tolerant Polar Gold arborvitae with Fluffy western arborvitae.

Thuja plicata FLUFFY®

Poolside Pot

CONTAINER TYPE **Faux-basket-weave resin planter with tapered sides**
CONTAINER SIZE **24 inches across × 12 inches deep** • SITE **Full sun**

YOUR POOL is the recreation center of your yard—make it the aesthetic focus as well. Lounging or entertaining friends on a poolside patio or deck will be even better with an exuberant, sun-loving container by your side.

The dwarf Egyptian papyrus Graceful Grasses Prince Tut evokes an aquatic theme and will make you feel like king or queen of the Nile with its 3- to 4-foot green scepters. Stout stems allow this annual grass to form an upright fountain of greenery without flopping. Nestled around the base of the papyrus are trailing mounds of Supertunia Vista Bubblegum petunias. The rose-veined, hot-pink blossoms supply a vivid contrast to the cool green of the papyrus. Hummingbirds and butterflies will flock to the petunias, too.

Gardener's Hint

Keep the papyrus well-watered, especially during the summer heat. Supertunia Vista Bubblegum is a vigorous grower and may become leggy by midsummer. Cut back the longest stems (no more than one fifth of the total) to the container's lip and fertilize to encourage strong and dense regrowth.

INGREDIENTS

A **1 DWARF EGYPTIAN PAPYRUS;** *Cyperus papyrus*
GRACEFUL GRASSES® PRINCE TUT™

B **4 PETUNIAS;** *Petunia* SUPERTUNIA VISTA®
BUBBLEGUM®

PLANTING GUIDE

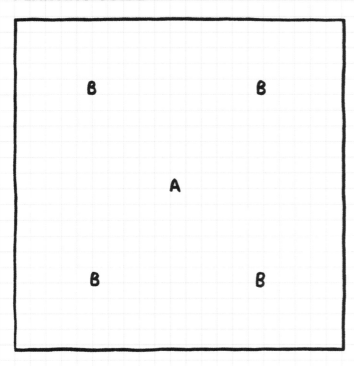

SUBSTITUTIONS

Superbena Sparkling Amethyst also
looks vibrant posed against the dwarf
Egyptian papyrus.

Verbena SUPERBENA
SPARKLING® Amethyst

In the Pink

CONTAINER TYPE **Ceramic bowl**
CONTAINER SIZE **12 inches across × 16 inches deep** • SITE **Full sun**

MAYBE PINK—the color of romance—is your favorite color, or maybe it just complements the color of your house or is part of the theme for a party. Whatever your reason for celebrating this hue, this single color arrangement will give you a new appreciation. Pinks run the gamut from soft to shocking. You'll discover how different shades deliver different effects in this monochromatic arrangement that contrasts one pink with another and another. Enjoy this recipe in any sunny spot, from late spring through early fall.

The focal point for this arrangement—the thriller—is a variegated red fountain grass (Graceful Grasses 'Fireworks'), which gushes up from the center of the container in a fountain of pink-striped leaves and paler pink bottlebrush flowers. It is surrounded by the complementary colors of Superbells Pink calibrachoas—with deep rose, funnel-shaped blooms—and Supertunia Trailing Strawberry Pink Veined, whose pink trumpets are intricately traced with darker pink veins. Spilling over the container's lip like a cerise avalanche is Superbena Sparkling Ruby. This festival of pinks is attractive to humans as well as butterflies and hummingbirds.

Gardener's Hint

By late summer, the calibrachoas and petunias may start to sprawl and thin out. If they do, shear the calibrachoa back to a few inches, but prune the petunia more selectively, cutting back one out of five shoots by approximately one fifth. Superbena verbenas normally remain dense without pruning and deadheading is not required.

INGREDIENTS

A **1 VARIEGATED RED FOUNTAIN GRASS;** *Pennisetum setaceum* GRACEFUL GRASSES® 'Fireworks'

B **2 CALIBRACHOAS;** *Calibrachoa* SUPERBELLS® Pink

C **2 PETUNIAS;** *Petunia* SUPERTUNIA® Trailing Strawberry Pink Veined

D **2 VERBENA;** *Verbena* SUPERBENA SPARKLING® Ruby

PLANTING GUIDE

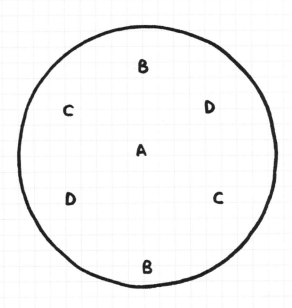

SUBSTITUTIONS

For another pink planting, situate Señorita Rosalita spider flower as the thriller. Surround with Karalee Petite Pink wand flower, Whirlwind fan flower, and Superbena Royale Cherryburst verbena.

Cleome SEÑORITA ROSALITA®

Gaura lindheimeri KARALEE® Petite Pink

Scaevola aemula WHIRLWIND® Pink

Verbena SUPERBENA ROYALE® Cherryburst

Sunnyside Up

CONTAINER TYPE Tapering ceramic planter
CONTAINER SIZE **15 inches across × 15 inches deep** • SITE **Full sun**

YELLOW IS THE MOST luminous color, a bright eye-catcher that warms us with a glance. This full-sun cocktail of yellows presents an enjoyable variety of hues and textures. Start with a mound of sunny Vanilla Butterfly marguerite daisies, then surround with the trailing stems and brilliant flowers of Superbells Yellow calibrachoas. Add a dash of palest Supertunia Limoncello to inject a cooling note, and you are done.

Bred for heat-tolerance and toughness, these floral gems will keep you in flowers all summer long, while also attracting quick, colorful hummingbirds.

Gardener's Hint

When summer nights grow hot, regularly staying in the high 70s or above, the bloom of the marguerite daisies may falter in spite of regular deadheading. If it does, trim the plant back by about one third with a sharp pair of scissors or pruning shears. This treatment will encourage new growth that will flower generously when the night temperatures drop.

INGREDIENTS

A **1 MARGUERITE DAISY;** *Argyranthemum frutescens*
VANILLA BUTTERFLY®

B **3 CALIBRACHOAS;**
Calibrachoa SUPERBELLS®
Yellow

C **3 PETUNIAS;** *Petunia*
SUPERTUNIA® LIMONCELLO®

PLANTING GUIDE

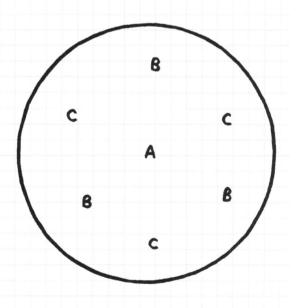

SUBSTITUTIONS

In regions where summers are long and hot, replace the marguerite daisy with a yellow gerbera daisy.

Gerbera yellow cultivar

Oh, Deer

CONTAINER TYPE **Rimmed plastic bowl**
CONTAINER SIZE **32 inches across × 12 inches deep** • SITE **Full sun**

NO PLANTING is truly deer-proof because if deer over-populate your region, they will eat virtually any plant. However, deer have their favorites, and the plants in this container are typically not to their taste, resulting in minimal browsing under most circumstances.

And happily you don't have to sacrifice beauty for safety. Lil' Miss Sunshine bluebeard furnishes shiny yellow, aromatic leaves throughout the growing season, backed up by an abundance of blue flowers along the stems from summer to autumn. Mounding annual Bandana Pink lantana is a continuous bloomer with butterfly-attracting clusters of small pink-and-cream flowers.

For best results, locate this container in a sunny spot, but one not frequented by pets—according to the Humane Society of America, lantana leaves can be toxic to pets.

Gardener's Hint

Lil' Miss Sunshine bluebeard produces shiny yellow, aromatic leaves throughout the growing season, backed up by clusters of blue purple flowers. It is a deciduous shrub that is hardy from USDA zone 5–9. In fall, when the rest of the plants in this container wither, transplant the bluebeard to a sunny, well-drained spot in the garden for years of rebloom.

INGREDIENTS

A **1 BLUEBEARD;** *Caryopteris ×clandonensis*
LIL' MISS SUNSHINE®

B **3 LANTANAS;** *Lantana camara* BANDANA® Pink

PLANTING GUIDE

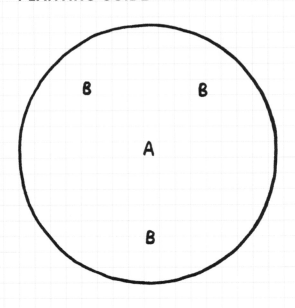

SUBSTITUTIONS

In the chillier parts of zone 5, Sunshine Blue II bluebeard may be a safer choice than Lil' Miss Sunshine. This extra cold-tolerant selection is better equipped to survive in colder regions over the long-term.

Caryopteris incana
SUNSHINE BLUE® II

Sunny Window Box

CONTAINER TYPE **Plastic window box**

CONTAINER SIZE **36 inches long** × **10 inches wide** × **12 inches deep** • SITE **Full sun**

Gardener's Hint

A west- or south-facing window is best for most abundant bloom, but know that with its extra exposure to the elements, a window box in a sunny location can get very hot, causing injury to plant roots. Wooden window boxes provide superior insulation; plastic is adequate except in hot climates. Another solution is to "double-pot," that is, to plant inside a slightly smaller container set inside the outer, visible one—isolating the inner container helps protect against overheating.

A WINDOW BOX is the quickest and easiest way to spruce up the façade of a house—just make sure the materials and colors of the box and house harmonize—and it maximizes the impact of the gardener's efforts by raising up the design to where it can't be overlooked. Window boxes are also a great opportunity for self-expression for gardeners with limited access to the soil, such as residents of a townhouse or condominium. Consider planting a window box outside a room you frequent often during the day, so that you can enjoy your planting from the inside as well as the outside.

Start by placing the grasses—Graceful Grasses 'Rubrum' fountain grass—at 12-inch intervals across the window box; these rosy fountains of foliage and flowers will anchor the arrangement. Drape the corners and center of the window box with vining Sweet Caroline Sweetheart Lime sweet potato vine to create flanking waterfalls of cool green hearts. Between the grasses and sweet potato vine insert Supertunia Bordeaux plants; these mounded annuals provide a contrasting form as well as season-long bloom of large, plummy-pink flowers veined with darker purple.

INGREDIENTS

A **2 PURPLE FOUNTAIN GRASSES;** *Pennisetum setaceum* GRACEFUL GRASSES® 'Rubrum'

B **3 SWEET POTATO VINES;** *Ipomoea* Sweet Caroline Sweetheart Lime

C **4 PETUNIAS;** *Petunia* SUPERTUNIA® BORDEAUX™

SUBSTITUTIONS

An alternative planting scheme with a similar effect would be a mixture of Angelface Wedgwood Blue summer snapdragons, 'Sweet Caroline Red' sweet potato vine, and Snowstorm Blue bacopa.

Angelonia ANGELFACE® Wedgwood Blue

Ipomoea batatas 'Sweet Caroline Red'

Sutera cordata SNOWSTORM® Blue

PLANTING GUIDE

```
┌──────────────────────────────────────────────┐
│                                                │
│      C                        C                │
│   B     A        B        A        B           │
│      C                        C                │
│                                                │
└──────────────────────────────────────────────┘
```

Complementary Contrast of Orange and Blue

CONTAINER TYPE **Faux-wood resin box**
CONTAINER SIZE **14 inches long × 12 inches wide × 7 inches deep** • SITE **Full sun**

WHEN IT COMES to personal wear, you may define clashing colors as a wardrobe malfunction, but a complementary contrast (as artists call it) can have an energizing effect when applied in controlled doses to the garden. Use this combination of orange and blue to wake up a sunny terrace, deck, or patio—the contrast of these flowers is truly vibrant.

Begin by planting an orange gerbera daisy in the center of the container where its bright orange flowers will show off to best effect. Tuck blue-flowered Blue My Mind dwarf morning glories in each corner, before flipping the switch back to orange with the Luscious Marmalade lantanas.

Gardener's Hint

When planting a design with such brightly colored flowers, it is important to use a container that does not compete with them. The rather plain faux-wooden container pictured fits the bill perfectly.

INGREDIENTS

A **1 GERBERA DAISY;**
Gerbera orange cultivar

B **4 DWARF MORNING GLORIES;**
Evolvulus BLUE MY MIND®

C **4 LANTANAS;** *Lantana camara*
LUSCIOUS® Marmalade

PLANTING GUIDE

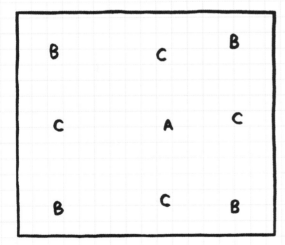

SUBSTITUTIONS

You can achieve a similar energizing effect in hot summer regions with a combination of yellow and purple, such as a singular yellow gerbera daisy surrounded by Superbells Yellow calibrachoas and Supertunia Trailing Blue petunias.

Gerbera yellow cultivar

Petunia SUPERTUNIA®
Trailing Blue

Calibrachoa SUPERBELLS®
Yellow

Succulent Container

CONTAINER TYPE **Tapering stone bowl**
CONTAINER SIZE **16 inches across × 6 inches deep** • SITE **Full sun**

SUCCULENTS ARE the camels of the plant world: the plants store water in their stems and leaves to keep hydrated during hot, dry weather. This makes them ideal for hot, drought-prone regions, and saves the gardener from the need for constant irrigation. Besides, they have a special, offbeat beauty all their own—anyone with a suitably sunny spot will want to decorate it with this arrangement.

A pair of brightly flowered moss roses—Mojave Fuchsia and Mojave Tangerine—surround Lemon Coral Mexican stonecrops. The stonecrops form dense, rounded cushions of fleshy chartreuse foliage rosettes with a fine, needle-like texture that contrasts pleasingly with the flat, rounded moss rose leaves.

INGREDIENTS

A **4 MOSS ROSES;** *Portulaca umbraticola* MOJAVE® Fuchsia

B **3 MOSS ROSES;** *Portulaca umbraticola* MOJAVE® Tangerine

C **3 MEXICAN STONECROPS;** *Sedum mexicanum* LEMON CORAL™

PLANTING GUIDE

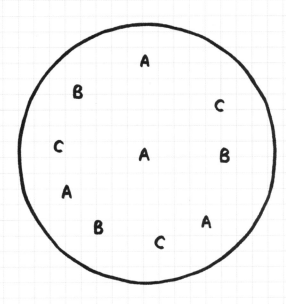

SUBSTITUTIONS

An alternative mix would be surrounding Lemon Coral with Rock 'N Grow Lemonjade autumn stonecrops and Mojave Yellow moss roses.

Sedum ROCK 'N GROW® 'Lemonjade'

Portulaca umbraticola MOJAVE® Yellow

Evening Magic

CONTAINER TYPE **Round ceramic planter**
CONTAINER SIZE **16.5 inches across × 17 inches deep** • SITE **Full sun**

WHEN TWILIGHT FALLS, most colors darken and fade into the background, but not the whites. Indeed, as the light fades, the white flowers in this container pop out of the darkness like glowing beacons. Though lacking color beyond green and white, this arrangement—which thrives in sun or part shade—offers plenty of contrast, in a sophisticated interplay of different flower sizes, forms, and textures.

Pure White Butterfly Marguerite daisy is the centerpiece anchoring the container. Superbena Whiteout, whose star-shaped flowers are borne in pure-white, crown-like clusters, spills over the container's edges. Like an encircling garland, mounds of Supertunia White, with its large white trumpets, intermingle with the airy, white mini-blossoms of Diamond Frost euphorbias.

Your guests won't be the only admirers of these evening performers. Their heightened visibility draws a special class of pollinators—moths who add their own ghostly element to the scene. A special bonus is petunia's fragrance, released at twilight to attract these late-flying visitors.

Gardener's Hint

The flowering of the marguerite daisy may stall if nighttime temperatures reach the high 70s or above on a regular basis. If this happens, cut the plant back with a sharp pair of shears—this treatment forces out new growth that will bloom prolifically when the temperature cools.

INGREDIENTS

A **1 MARGUERITE DAISY;** *Argyranthemum frutescens* PURE WHITE BUTTERFLY®

B **2 VERBENAS;** *Verbena* SUPERBENA® WHITEOUT™

C **2 PETUNIAS;** *Petunia* SUPERTUNIA® White

D **2 EUPHORBIAS;** *Euphorbia* DIAMOND FROST®

PLANTING GUIDE

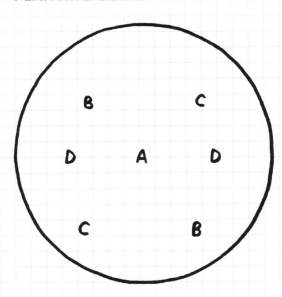

SUBSTITUTIONS

An alternative arrangement could feature a central Stratosphere White wand flower surrounded by Superbells White calibrachoas, Endless 'Flirtation' browallias, and 'Snow Princess' sweet alyssum.

Gaura lindheimeri STRATOSPHERE™ White

Calibrachoa SUPERBELLS® White

Browallia ENDLESS™ Flirtation

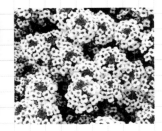

Lobularia SNOW PRINCESS®

Container Full of Perfumes

CONTAINER TYPE **Footed ceramic urn**
CONTAINER SIZE **16 inches across × 20 inches deep** • SITE **Full sun to part shade**

FRAGRANCE IS AN EXTRA dimension of pleasure that gardeners, preoccupied by flower color, often overlook. Yet it is uniquely evocative: scientists say that our sense of smell is directly connected to the parts of the brain that record and process memories. Here, though, you don't have to choose. This arrangement will gratify both the nose and the eye with its colorful, perfume-laden flowers.

Supertunia Sangria Charm is the lynchpin of this arrangement; it's a real eye-catcher with small but vivid raspberry trumpets, and a spreading habit. Superbena Royale Chambray—an upright, mounding plant with clusters of rich purple flowers—makes a lovely contrast. Fill in between and around with the intensely honey-scented flowers of the aptly named White Knight sweet alyssum.

Gardener's Hint

If the petunias and sweet alyssum grow leggy by midsummer, trim the stems back with a sharp pair of shears to prompt dense regrowth and a renewed burst of bloom.

INGREDIENTS

A **2 PETUNIAS;** *Petunia* SUPERTUNIA® Sangria Charm

B **2 VERBENAS;**
Verbena SUPERBENA
ROYALE® Chambray

C **2 SWEET ALYSSUM;**
Lobularia WHITE KNIGHT®

PLANTING GUIDE

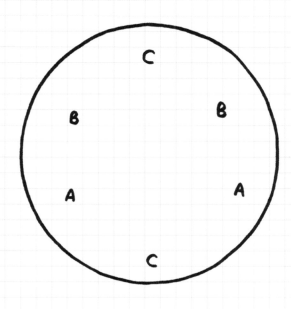

SUBSTITUTIONS

If the recommended ingredients should prove unavailable, substitute Supertunia Royal Velvet and Supertunia Pink Star Charm petunias, and Diamond Delight euphorbias.

Petunia SUPERTUNIA®
ROYAL VELVET®

Petunia SUPERTUNIA®
Pink Star Charm

Euphorbia DIAMOND
DELIGHT®

Best of the Blues

CONTAINER TYPE **Square plastic planter with rounded corners**
CONTAINER SIZE **18 inches across × 17 inches deep** • SITE **Full sun to part shade**

THE BLUES AREN'T EASY! There is no true blue pigment in flowers and as a result less than 10 percent of flowering plants manage to produce floral displays close to this color. This arrangement, however, features four of the best, enough to satisfy the most dedicated blues enthusiast and beautify any sunny or partially shaded spot.

The anchor or thriller for the arrangement is Let's Dance Blue Jangles hydrangea. This compact shrub bears big, rounded clusters of flowers in early summer and reblooms in mid and late summer, too. The blossoms can vary in color, but if you make sure to use an acidic fertilizer (a product recommended for hollies and other broadleaf evergreens) the hue should be heavenly.

Around the hydrangea arrange as fillers two flowers whose blues are enriched with just a slight purple tinge: Artist Blue flossflower and Whirlwind Blue fanflowers. Then weave in around the edge the spiller, Blue My Mind dwarf morning glories, whose flowers are indeed a startling shade of deep sky blue, set against soft, silvery leaves.

Gardener's Hint

The hydrangea is a deciduous shrub hardy from USDA zone 5–9. After the first fall frost puts an end to this container's display, transplant the hydrangea to a sunny or partially shaded spot in the garden where it should provide many years of additional enjoyment.

INGREDIENTS

A **1 HYDRANGEA;**
Hydrangea macrophylla
LET'S DANCE® BLUE
JANGLES®

B **4 FLOSSFLOWERS;**
Ageratum ARTIST® Blue

C **4 FAN FLOWERS;**
Scaevola aemula
WHIRLWIND BLUE®

D **4 DWARF MORNING
GLORIES;** *Evolvulus* BLUE
MY MIND®

PLANTING GUIDE

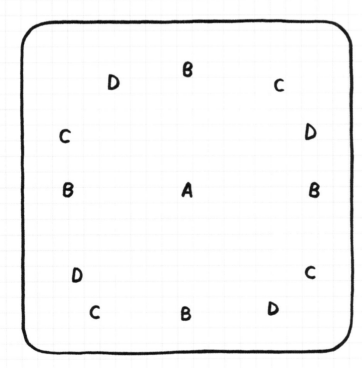

SUBSTITUTIONS

If you have trouble obtaining Let's
Dance Blue Jangles hydrangea, you can
substitute similarly hued Rockin' Playin'
The Blues salvia.

*Salvia longispicata
×farinacea* ROCKIN'®
PLAYIN' THE BLUES®

Seeing Red

CONTAINER TYPE Coco-lined hanging basket on a metal stand
CONTAINER SIZE **12 inches across** × **12 inches deep** • SITE **Full sun**

DESIGNERS DIVIDE COLORS into warm versus cool—cool colors are soothing and retiring, while warm colors are energizing and assertive. And surely, nothing is warmer than a real hot red. Flowers of this color seem to pop out of the landscape, irresistibly drawing your eye, especially as they contrast so vibrantly with the green of foliage. This particular arrangement features three hot reds, making it a powerful visual exclamation point, something that makes any sunny spot where you choose to place it center stage.

Certainly, the fiery trumpets of Supertunia Really Red blaze with color. The smaller, but no-less-intense blossoms of the red Superbells calibrachoas mingle and match their intensity. Superbena Scarlet Star displays its vivid flower heads against handsome, frilly, deep green foliage. Neither you nor the hummingbirds will be able to resist this container!

Gardener's Hint

Regular fertilization is a key to keeping this container in full, glorious bloom. Add a slow-release fertilizer at planting time and again in July. Whenever growth slows, supplement by applying a water-soluble fertilizer at irrigation time.

INGREDIENTS

A **2 PETUNIAS;** *Petunia* SUPERTUNIA®
Really Red

B **2 CALIBRACHOAS;** *Calibrachoa*
SUPERBELLS® Red

C **4 VERBENAS;**
Verbena SUPERBENA®
Scarlet Star

PLANTING GUIDE

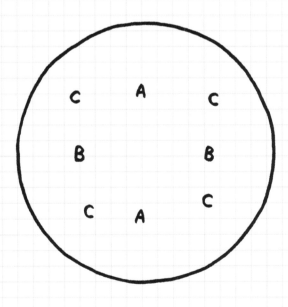

SUBSTITUTIONS

For a red container in a shady location, replace the petunias and calibrachoas with Artful Heartfire angel wings and Surefire Red begonias, and the verbenas with Infinity Red New Guinea impatiens.

Caladium hortulanum
ARTFUL® HEARTFIRE®

Begonia benariensis
SUREFIRE® Red

Impatiens hawkeri
INFINITY® Red

Black and White

CONTAINER TYPE **Footed metal urn**
CONTAINER SIZE **21 inches square × 28.5 inches deep** • SITE **Full sun**

NO PLANTS are truly black, but the midnight purples of this container's foliages come close and, when contrasted to the white blossoms, make a stylish statement for any sunny spot.

Vertigo pennisetum sets the tone with an upwelling of inky, grassy leaves at the container's center. Shining against this backdrop like stars in a dark sky are the pure white blossoms of Diamond Frost euphorbia; Supertunia Latte combines both colors in its white flowers veined with black coffee. Reiterating the black theme on opposite sides of the planting is *Ipomoea* Sweet Caroline Raven, whose vining stems and forked dark purple leaves spill over the container's edge like a sooty skirt.

Gardener's Hint

Because darker foliage absorbs the most sunlight, it is especially susceptible to wilting on sunny days, so it is particularly important to water this container conscientiously.

INGREDIENTS

A **1 PURPLE FOUNTAIN GRASS;** *Pennisetum purpureum* GRACEFUL GRASSES® VERTIGO®

B **2 EUPHORBIAS;** *Euphorbia* DIAMOND FROST®

C **4 PETUNIAS;** *Petunia* SUPERTUNIA® LATTE™

D **4 SWEET POTATO VINES;** *Ipomoea* Sweet Caroline Raven

PLANTING GUIDE

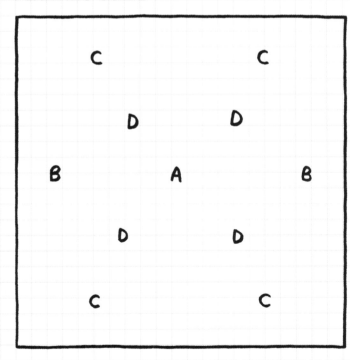

SUBSTITUTIONS

To make this container suitable for a partially shaded spot, replace the purple fountain grass with Primo 'Black Pearl' coral bells.

Heuchera PRIMO® 'Black Pearl'

Butterfly Magnet

CONTAINER TYPE **Round plastic pot (1)** • CONTAINER SIZE **16 inches across × 12 inches deep**

CONTAINER TYPE **Resin railing box (2)**
CONTAINER SIZE **15.5 inches long × 12 inches wide × 9.5 inches deep**

SITE **Full sun**

Gardener's Hint

Massed containers (such as called for here) are more effective at attracting butterflies than a single pot or basket. The prolonged bloom time of this arrangement also provides a sustained diet of pollen and nectar for visiting pollinators.

NOT ONE CONTAINER, BUT THREE! We've partnered a round container with a pair of railing boxes to create a butterfly magnet for the corner of a deck or porch. Any of the recommended plants is a major butterfly-attractor alone, but the result will be irresistible when combined in this triple-threat assortment. Your friends will also flock to admire this sun-loving symphony of color.

To plant the round pot, start with the Meteor Shower verbena. It has a denser, more vigorous growth habit than other tall verbenas; it's also more compact, as well as heat and drought tolerant, which makes it ideal for a container. Around the verbena alternate Goldilocks Rocks bidens and Luscious Berry Blend lantanas, both of which also tolerate heat and drought. Goldilocks Rocks produces its daisy-like yellow flowers all summer long without any need for deadheading; Berry Blend is also self-cleaning and has a light, sweet fragrance that butterflies and hummingbirds find irresistible.

The railing boxes get a simplified planting of Goldilocks Rocks bidens (one for each corner) with two Luscious Berry Blend lantanas arranged in the center of each box.

INGREDIENTS
In pot

A **1 VERBENA;** *Verbena bonariensis* METEOR SHOWER®

B **3 BIDENS;** *Bidens ferulifolia* GOLDILOCKS ROCKS®

C **3 LANTANAS;** *Lantana camara* LUSCIOUS® BERRY BLEND™

SUBSTITUTIONS

Those who prefer a darker, purple-based color scheme can replace the verbena with a Rock 'N Grow 'Maestro' autumn stonecrop, swap the bidens for Pardon My Purple bee balms, and substitute Luscious Grape lantanas for the Berry Blend.

Sedum ROCK 'N GROW® 'Maestro'

Monarda didyma 'Pardon My Purple'

Lantana montevidensis LUSCIOUS® Grape

In railing boxes

B 8 BIDENS (4 FOR EACH BOX);
Bidens ferulifolia GOLDILOCKS ROCKS®

C 4 LANTANAS (2 FOR EACH BOX);
Lantana camara LUSCIOUS® BERRY BLEND™

PLANTING GUIDE

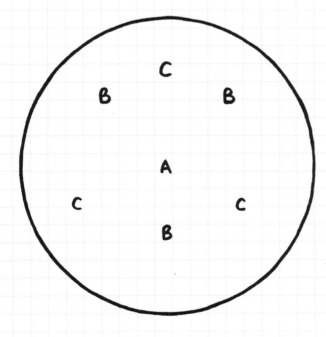

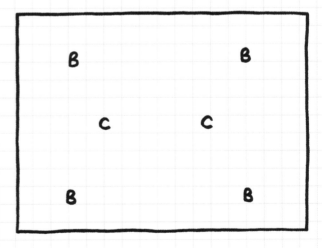

Resources

Finding Proven Winners plants in your local garden retailer is easy: look for the branded white pots marked with a large "PW" and prominent labels also marked "PW." Visit provenwinners.com (or provenwinners.eu) to learn more about all the plant possibilities, buy plants online, or find information about local retailers. The Bransford Webbs Plant Company, grower and supplier of Proven Winners shrubs, is a helpful resource for finding Proven Winners plants and retailers in the United Kingdom (bransfordwebbs.co.uk).

Here are a few other sources of reliable information—online and books—to help you start your garden.

ONLINE RESOURCES

Missouri Botanical Garden Plant Finder
  missouribotanicalgarden.org/plantfinder/plantfindersearch.aspx

USDA Cooperative Extension Directory
  nifa.usda.gov/land-grant-colleges-and-universities-partner
  -website-directory?state=All&type=Extension

USDA Plant Hardiness Zone Map
  planthardiness.ars.usda.gov/PHZMWeb/

BOOKS

Bennett, Pamela, and Maria Zampini. 2015. *Garden-pedia: An A-to-Z Guide to Gardening Terms*. Pittsburgh, PA: St. Lynn's Press.

Clausen, Ruth Rogers. 2011. *50 Beautiful Deer-Resistant Plants: The Prettiest Annuals, Perennials, Bulbs, and Shrubs that Deer Don't Eat*. Portland, OR: Timber Press.

Clausen, Ruth Rogers, and Thomas Christopher. 2015. *Essential Perennials: The Complete Reference to 2700 Perennials for the Home Garden*. Portland, OR: Timber Press

Cohen, Stephanie, and Jennifer Benner. *The Non-Stop Garden: A Step-by-Step Guide to Smart Plant Choices and Four-Season Designs*. Portland, OR: Timber Press.

Mendez, Kerry Ann. 2015. *The Right-Size Flower Garden: Simplify Your Outdoor Space with Smart Design Solutions and Plant Choices*. Pittsburgh, PA: St. Lynn's Press.

Richardson, Fern. 2012. *Small-Space Container Gardens: Transform Your Balcony, Porch, or Patio with Fruits, Flowers, Foliage, and Herbs*. Portland, OR: Timber Press.

Schmid, W. George. 2005. *Timber Press Pocket Guide to Shade Perennials*. Portland, OR: Timber Press.

Schwartz, Bobbie. 2017. *Garden Renovation: Transform Your Yard into the Garden of Your Dreams*. Portland, OR: Timber Press.

Wise, Barbara. 2012. *Container Gardening for All Seasons: Enjoy Year-Round Color with 101 Designs*. Nashville, TN: Cool Springs Press.

Acknowledgments

Many individuals assisted us with the production of this book. In particular, we would like to thank Jeff Huntington, Jessica Tatro, and their staff of Pleasant View Gardens in Loudon, NH, for all their efforts to turn our container and garden plans into reality, and thank you to Henry Huntington for allowing his home as a garden setting. Likewise, we owe a debt of thanks to Dale Deppe, president of Spring Meadow Nursery, Inc., for his hospitality; to Stacey Hirvela and Mark Osgerby of Spring Meadow Nursery, Inc., and Jeremy Windemuller, Windridge Perennials & Landscaping LLC, for their horticultural skill and patience; and to David Sparks for his photography. We appreciated the donation of containers by Barbara Wise of Crescent Gardens and Claudia Marshall of Gardeners Supply. Kerry Michaels, photographer extraordinaire, brought out the beauty intrinsic to every container. Marshall Dirks, Director of Marketing and Public Relations at Proven Winners was always supportive and shared his company's photographic resources.

Finally, our thanks to Andrew Beckman, Juree Sondker, Jacoba Lawson, all the personnel at Timber Press, and editor Mollie Firestone.

Photo and Illustration Credits

Index

ALAN DETRICK

RUTH ROGERS CLAUSEN

Ruth was trained at Studley Horticultural College in the United Kingdom and has been in the industry for several decades on both sides of the Atlantic. She has written several gardening books and lectures widely on a range of horticultural topics. In 1989 Random House published *Perennials for American Gardens* (co-authored with Nicolas H. Ekstrom); it received the GWA Gold Award; Hearst Books published *Dreamscaping* in 2003. Her book about successful gardening in deer country: *50 Beautiful Deer-Resistant Plants* (Timber Press, 2011) is in its seventh printing. *Essential Perennials*, co-authored with Thomas Christopher (Timber Press, 2015) has received excellent reviews. Ruth was horticulture editor for *Country Living Gardener* for more than seven years.

WILLIAM BURKHART

THOMAS CHRISTOPHER

A graduate of the New York Botanical Garden School of Professional Horticulture, Thomas Christopher worked for ten years as a horticulturist for Columbia University on an historic Hudson River estate. More recently, he has focused on writing about horticulture, publishing articles in a wide range of magazines and newspapers including *The New York Times*, *The Journal of the Royal Horticultural Society*, and *Horticulture Magazine*, as well as serving as a columnist for *House & Garden* and a contributing editor at *Martha Stewart Living*. He is also the author of more than a dozen gardening books, including *Essential Perennials* (co-authored with Ruth Rogers Clausen) and *Garden Revolution*, which he co-wrote with Larry Weaner and which was published in 2016.